# Contents

# The Paragraph

The paragraph! That's the working unit of both writer and reader. The writer works hard to put meaning into the paragraph; the reader works hard to take meaning out of it. Though they work at opposite tasks, the work of each is closely related. Actually, to understand better the job of the reader, one must first understand better the job of the writer. So, let us look briefly at the writer's job.

**One Main Idea.** To make their meaning clear, writers know that they must follow certain basic principles. First, they know that they must develop only one main idea per paragraph. This principle is so important that they know it backward too. They know that they must not try to develop two main ideas in the same paragraph.

**The Topic Sentence.** The next important principle they know is that each main idea can be stated in a topic sentence, and that such a sentence best serves its function by coming at or near the beginning of its paragraph. They know too, that the more clearly they can state the topic of a paragraph in the opening sentence, the more effective they will be in developing a meaningful, well-organized paragraph.

One word of warning to the reader: There is no guarantee that the topic sentence will always be the first sentence of a paragraph. Occasionally, a writer will start off with an introductory or a transitional sentence. Then, it us up to the reader to spot such a sentence, and recognize it for what it is.

The topic sentence may be placed in several other positions in a paragraph. It may be placed in the middle, or even at the very end. If it appears at the end, though it may still be a topic sentence in form, in terms of function, it is more rightfully a *restatement*. Whenever the end position is chosen, it is chosen to give the restatement especial emphasis.

Finally, a paragraph may not have a topic sentence in it at all. Some writers purposely leave out such sentences. But, in such cases, inferring a topic sentence may not be as difficult as it may first appear. Here's why. Many such professional writers actually do write topic sentences, but on separate scraps of paper. They then place one of the scraps at the head of a sheet and use the topic sentence to guide their thoughts in the construction of the paragraph. With the paragraph written and the topic sentence having served its purpose, the scrap is discarded. The end result is a paragraph without a visible topic sentence, but the paragraph, nonetheless, has embedded in it all the clues that an alert reader needs for making an accurate inference.

**Finding Meaning.** Actually, there is nothing especially important in recognizing or inferring a topic sentence for its own sake. The important thing is that the reader use the topic sentence as a quick means of establishing a focal point around which to cluster the meanings of the subsequent words and sentences that he or she reads. Here's the double-edged sword again: just as writers use topic sentences to provide focus and structure for presenting their meaning, so the perceptive reader can use the topic sentence for focus and structure to gain meaning.

Up to this point, the reader, having looked secretly over the writer's shoulder, should have learned two exceedingly valuable secrets: first, expect only one main idea in each paragraph; and secondly, use the topic sentence to discover the topic of each paragraph.

**Supporting the Main Idea.** Now, there is more to a writer's job than writing paragraphs that consist of only bare topic sentences and main ideas. The balance of the job deals with developing each main idea through the use of supporting material that amplifies and clarifies the main idea and, many times, makes it more vivid and memorable.

To support their main ideas, writers may use a variety of forms. One of the most common is the example. Examples help to illustrate the main idea. Other supporting materials are anecdotes, incidents, jokes, allusions, comparisons, contrasts, analogies, definitions, exceptions, logic, and so forth.

To summarize, the reader should have learned from the writer that a textbook-type paragraph usually contains these three elements: a topic sentence, a main idea, and supporting material. Knowing this, the reader should use the topic sentence to find the main idea. Everything other than the main idea is supporting material used to illustrate, amplify, and qualify the main idea. So the reader must be able to separate the main idea from the supporting material, yet see the relationship between them.

# To the Student

## The Six Types of Questions

In this book, the basic skills necessary for reading factual material are taught through the use of the following six types of questions: subject matter, main idea, supporting details, conclusion, clarifying devices, and vocabulary in context questions.

**Subject Matter.** This question looks easy and often is easy. But don't let that fool you into thinking it isn't important. The subject matter question can help you with the most important skill of all reading and learning: concentration. With it, you comprehend and learn. Without it, you fail.

Here is the secret for gaining concentration: After reading the first few lines of something, ask yourself, "What is the subject matter of this passage?" Instantly, you will be thinking about the passage. You will be concentrating. If you don't ask this question, your eyes will move across the lines of print, yet your mind will be thinking of other things.

By asking this question as you read each passage in this book, you will master the skill so well that it will carry over to everything you read.

Let's see how this method works. Here is a short passage:

> The owl cannot move its eyes. The eyes are fixed in their sockets by strong muscles. But to make up for this drawback, nature gave the owl a special kind of neck. This neck allows the owl to turn its head in almost a full circle. It can do this without moving the rest of its body.

On finishing the first sentence your thought should have been something like, "Ah, a passage about the owl. Perhaps I'll learn some secret of the wise old bird." If it was, your head was in the right place. By focusing right away on the subject matter, you'll be concentrating, you'll be looking for something, your attitude will be superb, and best of all, you'll be understanding, learning, and remembering.

**Main Idea.** In reading anything, once you have grasped the subject matter, ask yourself, "What point is the writer trying to make?" Once you ask this question, your mind will be looking for an answer, and chances are that you will find one. But if you don't focus in this way, all things seem equal. Nothing stands out.

Try to find the main idea in the following passage by asking, "What point is the writer trying to make?"

> As an orange tree gets older, its fruit improves. Young trees bear fruit that has a thick rind and many seeds. As the tree becomes older, however, the skins become thinner and the fruit becomes much juicer. The seeds decrease in number. Some old, neglected trees bear fruit with a thin skin and luscious flavor. Some orange trees growing in the Azores bear fruit until they are 100 years old. They produce a highly prized fruit that is thin skinned, full of juice, and free from seeds.

A good answer is, "As an orange tree gets older its fruit gets better." This passage is fairly easy to figure out because the first sentence is an excellent topic sentence.

The next example does not have a topic sentence. Nevertheless, the question "What point is the writer trying to make?" can still be answered. This time, think about the passage and come up with your own answer.

> Did you ever wonder how much salt is contained in seawater? Here's a simple experiment you might want to try. Take a box six inches deep. Fill it with seawater. Allow the water to evaporate. There will be about two inches of salt left in the bottom of the box. Just think, if all the seawater on the earth evaporated, it would leave a layer of salt about 230 feet thick!

This passage may have required a bit more thought, for the correct answer is a summary type answer. Compare your answer with the following main idea statement: "Seawater has a large amount of salt in it."

**Supporting Details.** In common usage, the word *detail* has taken on the unrespected meaning of "something relatively unimportant." But details are important. Details are the plaster, board, and brick of a building, while main ideas are the large, strong steel or wooden beams. A solid, well-written passage must contain both.

The bulk of a factual passage is made up of details that support the main idea. The main idea is often buried among the details. You have to dig to distinguish between them. Here are some characteristics that can help you see the difference between supporting details and main ideas.

First, supporting details come in various forms, such as examples, explanations, descriptions, definitions, comparisons, contrasts, exceptions, analogies, similes, and metaphors.

Second, these various kinds of details are used to support the main idea. The words themselves, supporting details, spell out their job. So when you have trouble finding the main idea, take a passage apart sentence by sentence, asking, "Does this sentence support something, or is this the thing being supported?" In other words, you must not only separate the two, but also see how they help one another. The main idea can often be expressed in a single sentence. But a sentence cannot tell a complete story. The writer must use additional sentences to give you the full picture.

The following passage shows how important details are for providing a full picture of what the writer had in mind.

> Many of the first houses in America were made of bricks taken from ships. Ships, of course, weren't made of brick, but they often carried bricks as ballast. Ballast is heavy material put in the bottom of ships to keep them steady in the water. If a ship is heavier on the top than on the bottom, it is in trouble. The ship will tip over. Many of the ships that came to this country when it was young were almost empty except for bricks and sailors. The sailors knew that they could fill their empty ships with goods from the New World. When the ships arrived in America, their bricks were unloaded and sold. The sailors then had room to put goods from America in the ships' holds in place of the bricks.

Here we have the main idea in one sentence—the first sentence. Having stated the main idea, the writer goes on to explain why the bricks were used in ships and how they ended up being used to build houses. All of the sentences that tell us this information are giving us supporting details.

**Conclusion.** Some passages contain conclusions. Others do not. It all depends on the writer's purpose. For example, some passages describe a process—how something is done. There is no sense in trying to draw a conclusion from such a passage.

There are two kinds of passages with conclusions. In one, the conclusion is stated by the author. In the other, the conclusion is merely implied by the author. That is, the author seems to have come to a conclusion, but has not stated it. It is up to you to draw that conclusion.

Look for the conclusion that is stated in the following passage.

> The Earth's atmosphere cuts off all but about 47 percent of the sun's radiation. This is enough to warm our planet but not enough to make it boiling hot. The same heat keeps the earth warm after sunset. The warmth is trapped in the atmosphere, which acts like a blanket to keep us warm. It helps to keep temperatures from falling off too quickly after dark.

The author's conclusion is that the Earth's atmosphere acts like a blanket to keep the planet warm.

In the next excerpt, the author strongly implies a conclusion, but does not state it directly.

The great enemy of the earthworm is the mole. The pewit bird knows this. In order to make the worms think that a mole is near, the pewit taps the ground with one leg. The worms feel a vibration, or shaking motion, in the earth and think it's a mole. They then make their way to the surface to escape. There the pewit waits to snatch its prey.

From the above excerpt, we can draw the conclusion that the pewit is an intelligent bird.

Looking for a conclusion puts you in the shoes of a detective. While reading, you have to think, "Where is the writer leading me? What's the conclusion?" And, like a detective, you must try to guess the conclusion, changing the guess as you get more and more information.

**Clarifying Devices.** Clarifying devices are words, phrases, and techniques that a writer uses to make main ideas, sub-ideas, and supporting details clear and interesting. By knowing some of these clarifying and controlling devices, you will be better able to recognize them in the passages you read. By recognizing them, you will be able to read with greater comprehension and speed.

Two literary devices that make a writer's ideas both clear and interesting are similes and metaphors. Both are used to make comparisons that add color and power to ideas. An example of a simile is "She has a mind like a computer." In this simile, a person's mind is compared to a computer. A simile always uses the words *like, as,* or *than* to make a comparison. The metaphor, on the other hand, makes a direct comparison: "Her mind is a computer." Because metaphors are shorter and more direct, they are more forceful than similes. Writers use them to capture your attention, touch your emotions, and spark your imagination.

The largest single group of clarifying devices, and the most widely used, are transitional or signal words. For example, here are some signal words that you see all the time: *first, second, next, last, finally.* A writer uses such words to keep ideas, steps in a process, or lists in order. Other transitional words include *in brief, in conclusion, above all, therefore, since, because,* and *consequently.*

Organizational patterns are also clarifying devices. One such pattern is the chronological pattern, in which events unfold in the order of time: one thing happens first, then another, and another, and so on. A time pattern orders events. The event may take place in five minutes or over a period of hundreds of years.

**Vocabulary in Context.** How accurate are you in using words you think you already know? Do you know that the word *exotic* means "a thing or person from a foreign country?" So, exotic flowers and exotic dancers are flowers and dancers from a foreign country. *Exotic* has been used incorrectly so often and for so long that it has developed a second meaning. Most people use *exotic* to mean "strikingly unusual, as in color or design."

Many people think that the words *imply* and *infer* mean the same thing. They do not. An author may imply, or suggest, something. The reader then infers what the author implied. In other words, to imply is to suggest an idea. To infer is to take meaning out.

It would be easy to see what would happen to a passage if a reader skipped a word or two that he or she did not know, and imposed fuzzy meanings on a few others. The result would inevitably be a gross misunderstanding of the author's message. You will become a better reader if you learn the exact meanings and different shades of meaning of the words that are already familiar to you.

## Answering the Main Idea Question

The main idea questions in this book are not the usual multiple-choice variety from which you must select the one correct statement. Rather, you are given three statements and are asked to select the statement that expresses the main idea of the passage, the statement that is too narrow, and the statement that is too broad. You have to work hard and actively to identify all three statements correctly. This new type of question teaches you the differences among statements that, at first, seem almost equal.

To help you handle these questions, let's go behind the scenes to see how the main idea questions in this book were constructed. The true main idea statement was always written first. It had to be neat, succinct, and positive. The main idea tells who or what the subject of the passage is. It also answers the question does what? or is what? Next, keeping the main idea statement in mind, the other two statements were written. They are variations of the main idea statement. The too narrow statement had to be in line with the main idea, but express only part of it. Likewise, the too broad statement had to be in line with the main idea, but to be too general in scope.

Read the sample passage that starts below. Then, to learn how to answer the main idea questions, follow the instructions in the box. The answer to each part of the question has been filled in for you. The score for each answer has also been marked.

*Sample Passage*

Silk is fancy cloth that is much softer than cotton. Silk is made by the silkworm caterpillar. When full grown, the caterpillar weaves a cocoon of silk strands. It makes a sticky gum to hold the threads together. Long ago, in ancient China, people discovered how to wash the gum away. This made it possible for them to unwind the silk threads and weave them into cloth. The shimmering fabric could be dyed many colors. The process of making silk fabric was a Chinese secret for 2000 years. The Chinese sold silk to the rest of the world. But silkworms were eventually smuggled out of China. Now silk is made in many places around the world. The tiny silkworm is now part of a big industry.

| Main Idea | 1 | | Answer | Score |
|---|---|---|---|---|
| | **Mark the *main idea*** | | **M** | 15 |
| | **Mark the statement that is *too broad*** | | **B** | 5 |
| | **Mark the statement that is *too narrow*** | | **N** | 5 |

a. Silkworms make silk thread that can be woven into beautiful cloth.　　**M**　　15

[This statement is the main idea. It gathers all the important points of the passage. It tells (1) that the passage is about the silkworm, (2) that the silkworm makes silk thread, and (3) that the thread is woven into beautiful cloth.]

b. Silkworms make silk.　　**B**　　5

[This statement is too broad. Although the sentence is true, it leaves out some important points. We don't know (1) what form the silk takes when it is made, or (2) what the silk is used for.]

c. Silkworms spin silk cocoons.　　**N**　　5

[This sentence is too narrow. It tells us only part of the story. It completely ignores the fact that the silkworm's silk is made into cloth.]

## Getting the Most Out of This Book

The following steps could be called "tricks of the trade." Your teachers might call them "rules for learning." It doesn't matter what they are called. What does matter is that they work.

**Think About the Title.** A famous language expert told me a "trick" to use when I read. "The first thing to do is to read the title. Then spend a few moments thinking about it."

Writers spend much time thinking up good titles. They try to pack a lot of meaning into them. It makes sense, then, for you to spend a few seconds trying to dig out some meaning. These few moments of thought will give you a head start on a passage.

Thinking about the title can help you in another way, too. It helps you concentrate on a passage before you begin reading. Why does this happen? Thinking about the title fills your head full of thoughts about the passage. There's no room for anything else to get in to break concentration.

**The Dot System.** Here is a method that will speed up your reading. It also builds comprehension at the same time.

Spend a few moments with the title. Then read quickly through the passage. Next, without looking back, answer the six questions by placing a dot in the box next to each answer of your choice. The dots will be your "unofficial" answers. For the main idea question (question one) place your dot in the box next to the statement that you think is the main idea.

The dot system helps by making you think hard on your first, fast reading. The practice you gain by trying to grasp and remember ideas makes you a stronger reader.

**The Check-Mark System.** First, answer the main idea question. Follow the steps that are given above each set of statements for this question. Use a capital letter to mark your final answer to each part of the main idea question.

You have answered the other five questions with a dot. Now read the passage once more carefully. This time, mark your final answer to each question by placing a check mark (✓) in the box next to the answer of your choice. The answers with the check marks are the ones that will count toward your score.

**The Diagnostic Chart.** Now move your final answers to the Diagnostic Chart that starts on page 209.

Use the row of boxes beside Passage 1 for the answers to the first passage. Use the row of boxes beside Passage 2 for the answers to the second passage, and so on. Write the letter of your answer to the left of the dotted line in each block.

Correct your answers using the Answer Key on pages 203–207. When scoring your answers, do not use an x for incorrect or a c for correct. Instead, use this method. If your choice is incorrect, write the letter of the correct answer to the right of the dotted line in the block.

Thus, the row of answers for each passage will show your incorrect answers. And it will also show the correct answers.

**Your Total Comprehension Score.** Go back to the passage you have just read. If you answered a question incorrectly, draw a line under the correct choice on the question page. Then write your score for each question on the line provided. Add the scores to get your total comprehension score. Enter that number in the box marked Total Score.

**Graphing Your Progress.** After you have found your total comprehension score, turn to the Progress Graph that begins on page 215. Write your score in the box under the number of the passage. Then put an x along the line above the box to show your total comprehension score. Join the x's as you go. This will plot a line showing your progress.

**Taking Corrective Action.** Your incorrect answers give you a way to teach yourself how to read better. Take the time to study your wrong answers.

Go back to the questions. For each Question you got wrong, read the correct answer (the one you have underlined) several times. With the correct answer in mind, go back to the passage itself. Read to see why the approved answer is better. Try to see where you made your mistake. Try to figure out why you chose a wrong answer.

## The Steps in a Nutshell

Here's a quick review of the steps to follow. Following these steps is the way to get the most out of this book. Be sure you have read and understood everything in the "To the Student" section on pages ix–xvii before you start.

1. **Think About the Title of the Passage.** Try to get all the meaning the writer put into it.
2. **Read the Passage Quickly.**
3. **Answer the Questions, Using the Dot System.** Use dots to mark your unofficial answers. Don't look back at the passage.
4. **Read the Passage Again—Carefully.**
5. **Mark Your Final Answers.** Put a check mark (✔) in the box to note your final answer. Use capital letters for each part of the main idea question.

6. **Mark Your Answers on the Diagnostic Chart.** Record your final answers on the Diagnostic Chart that begins on page 209. Write your answers to the left of the dotted line in the answer blocks for the passage.

7. **Correct Your Answers.** Use the Answer Key on pages 203–207. If an answer is not correct, write the correct answer in the right side of the block, beside your wrong answer. Then go back to the question page. Place a line under the correct answer.

8. **Find Your Total Comprehension Score.** Find this by adding up the points you earned for each question. Enter the total in the box marked Total Score.

9. **Graph Your Progress.** Enter and plot your score on the graph that begins on page 215.

10. **Take Corrective Action.** Read your wrong answers. Read the passage once more. Try to figure out why you were wrong.

# To the Instructor

## The Reading Passages

Each of the 100 passages included in the book had to meet the following three criteria: high interest level, appropriate readability level, and factual content.

The high interest level was assured by choosing passages of mature content that would appeal to a wide range of readers.

The passages in *Six-Way Paragraphs, Introductory Level* range from reading level 1 through reading level 4, with 25 passages at each level. *Six-Way Paragraphs, Middle Level* contains passages that range from reading level 4 to reading level 8, with 20 passages at each reading level. The passages in *Six-Way Paragraphs, Advanced Level* range from reading level 8 to reading level 12, with 20 passages at each reading level.

The factual content was a definite requirement because by reading factual passages students build not only their reading skills but, of equal importance, their informational backgrounds.

## The Six Questions

This book is organized around six essential questions. The most important of these is the main idea question, which is actually a set of three statements. Students must first choose and label the statement that expresses the main idea of the passage; then they must label each of the other statements as being either too narrow or too broad to be the main idea.

In addition to the main idea question, there are five other questions. These questions are within the framework of the following five categories: subject matter, supporting details, conclusions, clarifying devices, and vocabulary in context.

By repeated practice with the questions within these six categories, students will develop an active, searching attitude that will carry over to the reading of other expository prose. These six types of questions will help them become aware of what they are reading at the time they are actually seeing the words and phrases on a page. This type of thinking-while-reading sets the stage for higher comprehension and better retention.

## The Diagnostic Chart

The Diagnostic Chart provides the most dignified form of guidance yet devised. With this chart, no one has to point out a student's weaknesses. The chart does that automatically, yielding the information directly and personally to the student, making self-teaching possible. The organization of the questions and the format for marking answers on the chart are what make it work so well.

The six questions for each passage are always in the same order. For example, the question designed to teach the skill of drawing conclusions is always the fourth question, and the main idea question is always first. Keeping the questions in a set order sets the stage for the smooth working of the chart.

The chart works automatically when students write the letter of their answer choices for each passage in the spaces provided. Even after completing only one passage, the chart will reveal the type or types of questions answered correctly, as well as the types answered incorrectly. As the answers for more passages are recorded, the chart will show the types of questions that are missed consistently. A pattern can be seen after three or more passages have been completed. For example, if a student answers question 4 (drawing conclusions) incorrectly for three out of four passages, the student's weakness in this area shows up automatically.

Once a weakness is revealed, have your students take the following steps: First, turn to the instructional pages in the beginning of the book, and study the section in which the topic is discussed. Second, go back and reread the questions that were missed in that particular category. Then, with the correct answer to a question in mind, read the entire passage again, trying to see how the author developed the answer to the question. Do this for each question that was missed. Third, when reading future passages, make an extra effort to correctly answer the questions in that particular category. Fourth, if the difficulty continues, arrange to see the instructor.

# 1 Feathery Homes

Did you know that there is a kind of bird that can sew? This bird, called the tailor-bird, uses its beak as a needle. It sews leaves together in the shape of a cup. Then it lines the cup with straw and lays its eggs there.

Each species builds its own special kind of nest. The most common materials used for nests are grasses, twigs, and feathers. A bird must weave these materials into a nest. Imagine building a house without cement or nails to hold it together!

A weaverbird builds a nest that looks like a basket. The nest is shaped like a pear with a hole in the middle. The hole is the door of the nest.

The ovenbird makes a nest that is very solid. The nest is made of mud. Like a sculptor, the ovenbird <u>molds</u> the mud into the shape of an oven and then lets it dry in the sun. The sun bakes the mud, making it very hard.

Not all birds make their homes in branches. Some birds build their nests on the ground, while others bury their eggs under the ground. And some birds do not build nests at all. For example, a bird called the fairy tern lays its eggs right on a branch. It tiptoes on the branch and balances its eggs very carefully so they won't fall. So, when you look for nests and eggs in the branches of trees and bushes, remember that some nests may be right under your feet!

| Main Idea | 1 | Answer | Score |
|---|---|---|---|
| | Mark the *main idea* | M | 15 |
| | Mark the statement that is *too broad* | B | 5 |
| | Mark the statement that is *too narrow* | N | 5 |

a. Some birds build their nests on the ground. ☐ _____

b. Each type of bird builds a special kind of nest. ☐ _____

c. There are many species of birds. ☐ _____

**Score 15 points for each correct answer.**          Score

**Subject Matter**  2  This passage centers on
- ☐ a. the many kinds of birds.
- ☐ b. the building of bird nests.
- ☐ c. the ovenbird.
- ☐ d. unusual birds.                                    _____

**Supporting Details**  3  The ovenbird builds its nest of
- ☐ a. straw.
- ☐ b. grass.
- ☐ c. mud.
- ☐ d. twigs.                                            _____

**Conclusion**  4  The writer of this passage admires
- ☐ a. the bright colors of the tailorbird.
- ☐ b. birds that bury their eggs.
- ☐ c. the basket-shaped nest of the weaverbird.
- ☐ d. the effort it takes to build a nest.              _____

**Clarifying Devices**  5  The writer compares the ovenbird to a
- ☐ a. tailor.
- ☐ b. sculptor.
- ☐ c. weaver.
- ☐ d. carpenter.                                        _____

**Vocabulary in Context**  6  The word <u>molds</u> means
- ☐ a. weaves.
- ☐ b. shapes.
- ☐ c. pours.
- ☐ d. gathers.                                          _____

**Add your scores for questions 1–6. Enter the total here and on the graph on page 215.**          Total Score          _____

3

# 2 Outsmarting the Enemy

When a garden warbler sings from trees or bushes, no one can see it. The colors of this songbird match the colors of the leaves. When an animal blends in with its surroundings, its enemies can't see it either. This kind of protection is called *camouflage*.

Birds must protect themselves from their enemies. Sometimes this means having to fight. Sometimes it means fooling the enemy. Sometimes it means being able to escape. Birds must also protect their eggs and their young. Cats, rats, and foxes love eggs for breakfast. They prowl around looking for eggs and young chicks to eat. How can birds defend themselves against such enemies?

Each species has its own way of defending itself. Birds called common terns fight with their beaks and claws. In a <u>swarm</u>, they peck and scratch at anyone who comes too close to their nests. Ostriches protect themselves by escaping. They can't fly, but they can run very fast on their long, muscular legs. These birds can reach speeds of up to forty miles per hour. How fast is that? Well, if the wind blows this hard, it can rip huge branches from trees.

A bird called a killdeer has a lot of courage. It cares very much for its young. It would rather die than see its eggs eaten by a fox. If a fox wanders toward the nest, the killdeer pretends to be hurt. Dragging one wing, it hops away from the nest and draws the hungry fox after it.

| Main Idea | 1 | | |
|---|---|---|---|
| | | **Answer** | **Score** |
| | Mark the *main idea* | M | 15 |
| | Mark the statement that is *too broad* | B | 5 |
| | Mark the statement that is *too narrow* | N | 5 |
| | a. All birds try to avoid their enemies. | ☐ | ___ |
| | b. Birds have many ways of defending themselves. | ☐ | ___ |
| | c. The ostrich defends itself best by running fast. | ☐ | ___ |

**Score 15 points for each correct answer.**      Score

**Subject Matter**    **2**    This passage is concerned with
- ☐ a. songbirds.
- ☐ b. foxes.
- ☐ c. bird defense.
- ☐ d. hiding.      _____

**Supporting Details**    **3**    The killdeer tricks the fox by
- ☐ a. feeding him eggs.
- ☐ b. pretending to be hurt.
- ☐ c. flying away.
- ☐ d. changing color.      _____

**Conclusion**    **4**    We can conclude from this passage that the killdeer
- ☐ a. wants its babies to survive.
- ☐ b. gets hurt easily.
- ☐ c. hops on one leg.
- ☐ d. pretends to like foxes.      _____

**Clarifying Devices**    **5**    "If the wind blows this hard, it can rip huge branches from the trees" refers to the ostrich's
- ☐ a. strength.
- ☐ b. temper.
- ☐ c. speed.
- ☐ d. power.      _____

**Vocabulary in Context**    **6**    A <u>swarm</u> is a
- ☐ a. cluster.
- ☐ b. nest.
- ☐ c. tree.
- ☐ d. frenzy.      _____

**Add your scores for questions 1–6. Enter the total here and on the graph on page 215.**      **Total Score**      _____

# 3 Rain Forests

Tropical rain forests grow near the equator, in the hottest parts of the world. Rain forests are always wet. The moisture just never dries up.

The trees in a rain forest are very tall and have very few limbs. The leaves are all at the top. They form a high ceiling. Very little sunlight comes through the leaves. Inside a rain forest it is as dark and quiet as a church.

There are very few low-growing plants on the rain forest floor. Walking through a rain forest is like being at a circus's high trapeze show—the most exciting things are happening high above the ground. Monkeys swing on vines, with baby monkeys on their backs. Large snakes crawl from branch to branch. Giant bats make squeaky noises.

The animals that stay near the ground are <u>fascinating</u>, too. The gentle tapir, which looks like a small horse with a long nose, covers itself with mud from head to foot. When the mud dries, it forms a kind of armor. It protects the tapir from biting insects. Another ground animal is the anteater. It has a long, sticky tongue that works like a fly trap. But the tongue is really an ant trap. For breakfast, lunch, and dinner the anteater eats nothing but ants, ants, and more ants!

| Main Idea | 1 | | Answer | Score |
|---|---|---|---|---|
| | **Mark the *main idea*** | | **M** | 15 |
| | **Mark the statement that is *too broad*** | | **B** | 5 |
| | **Mark the statement that is *too narrow*** | | **N** | 5 |

a. Many animals in the rain forest stay high in the trees. ☐ _____

b. A rain forest is a home for many interesting animals. ☐ _____

c. Many interesting animals live in tropical climates. ☐ _____

## Score 15 points for each correct answer.     Score

**Subject Matter**  **2**  This passage is mainly about
- ☐ a. trees.
- ☐ b. tropical rain forests.
- ☐ c. anteaters.
- ☐ d. monkeys.                              _____

**Supporting Details**  **3**  Mud protects the tapir from
- ☐ a. monkeys.
- ☐ b. anteaters.
- ☐ c. the heat.
- ☐ d. biting insects.                       _____

**Conclusion**  **4**  It is probable that few plants grow on the rain forest floor because
- ☐ a. there is not enough light.
- ☐ b. most animals are in the trees.
- ☐ c. there is not enough water.
- ☐ d. it is too hot.                         _____

**Clarifying Devices**  **5**  The activity in a rain forest is compared to
- ☐ a. a zoo.
- ☐ b. a church.
- ☐ c. a circus trapeze show.
- ☐ d. a tropical pet shop.                   _____

**Vocabulary in Context**  **6**  A <u>fascinating</u> animal is
- ☐ a. dangerous
- ☐ b. interesting
- ☐ c. frightening
- ☐ d. active.                                _____

**Add your scores for questions 1–6. Enter the total here and on the graph on page 215.**     **Total Score**     _____

**7**

# 4 Put a Lid on It

Sports have always been ruled by the weather. Rain, sleet, snow, and cold called the plays. Baseball fans often sat in the rain without cover, waiting for the sun to come out and the game to begin. Football lovers sometimes took days to warm up after sitting through a freezing cold Sunday game. For both sports fans and players, the domed stadium was like something out of a dream. A huge plastic bubble kept out rain and snow. There was heat to keep things comfortable year round.

Domed stadiums have clearly changed the <u>course</u> of sports. Still, they did have their problems at first. Most of these problems were discovered and solved at the Houston Astrodome. This was the world's first stadium with a lid. For the fans, it was great. But there were some problems for the players. Baseball outfielders had the most difficult time. They had to learn to catch in a field with a roof. At first this was almost as difficult as playing in the dark. The panes of the roof were light colored, to let sunlight in. Sunlight was needed to keep the grass on the field alive. But the light roof blended too well with the white baseball. Fly balls seemed to drop out of nowhere. Even skilled fielders were making errors. Finally, the decision was made to paint the panes of the roof dark. The problem was solved. What about the grass? Well, the real grass was dug up and replaced with artificial turf!

| Main Idea | 1 | | Answer | Score |
|---|---|---|:---:|:---:|
| | **Mark the *main idea*** | | M | 15 |
| | **Mark the statement that is *too broad*** | | B | 5 |
| | **Mark the statement that is *too narrow*** | | N | 5 |

a. Over the years there have been improvements that have made watching sports more comfortable. ☐ _____

b. The domed stadium made it possible for sports to be played in any weather. ☐ _____

c. Baseball and football fans used to suffer if the weather was bad. ☐ _____

**Score 15 points for each correct answer.**     **Score**

**Subject Matter**  **2**  This passage is about
☐ a. baseball games.
☐ b. cold weather.
☐ c. how to play outfield.
☐ d. domed stadiums.     _____

**Supporting Details**  **3**  At first, domed stadiums were especially difficult for
☐ a. baseball players.
☐ b. football players.
☐ c. fans.
☐ d. team owners.     _____

**Conclusion**  **4**  We can conclude that domed stadiums are
☐ a. a thing of the past.
☐ b. a passing fad.
☐ c. causing many changes in sports.
☐ d. expensive to keep up.     _____

**Clarifying Devices**  **5**  The literary device called *hyperbole* is an exaggerated statement. Choose the hyperbole from the examples below.
☐ a. Sports have always been ruled by the weather.
☐ b. Football lovers sometimes took days to warm up after a freezing cold Sunday game.
☐ c. It was the world's first stadium with a lid.
☐ d. At first this was almost as difficult as playing in the dark.     _____

**Vocabulary in Context**  **6**  In this passage the word <u>course</u> means
☐ a. a place for a race.
☐ b. a school of study.
☐ c. the direction.
☐ d. part of a meal.     _____

**Add your scores for questions 1–6. Enter the total here and on the graph on page 215.**     **Total Score**     _____

# 5 Two Unhappy Firsts

People enjoy talking about "firsts." They like to remember their first love or their first car. But not all firsts are happy ones. Some involve accidents or other sad events. Few people enjoy recalling the firsts that are bad.

One of history's bad but important firsts was the first car accident. Autos were still young when it happened. The crash took place in New York City. The year was 1896. The month was May. A man from Massachusetts was visiting the city in his new car. At the time, bicycle riders were still trying to get used to the new sets of wheels on the road.

In the accident, no one is sure who was at fault. In any case, the bike and the car <u>collided</u>. The man on the bike was injured. The driver of the car had to stay in jail and wait for the hospital report on the bicycle rider. Luckily, the rider was not killed.

Three years later, another automobile first took place. The scene was again New York City. A real estate broker named Henry Bliss stepped off a streetcar. He was hit by a passing car. Once again, no one is sure just how it happened or whose fault it was. The driver of the car was put in jail. Poor Mr. Bliss became the first person to die in a car accident.

| Main Idea | 1 | Answer | Score |
|---|---|---|---|
| | **Mark the _main idea_** | M | 15 |
| | **Mark the statement that is _too broad_** | B | 5 |
| | **Mark the statement that is _too narrow_** | N | 5 |

a. Not all firsts are happy firsts. ☐ _____

b. The first car accident and the first death from a car accident are two very unhappy "firsts." ☐ _____

c. It took bicycle riders a while to get used to cars on the road. ☐ _____

**Score 15 points for each correct answer.**            **Score**

**Subject Matter**    **2**    This passage is about
- ☐ a. the first bicycle accident.
- ☐ b. accidents in large cities.
- ☐ c. two of the first auto accidents.
- ☐ d. the first vehicles with wheels.      _____

**Supporting Details**    **3**    In each accident the driver was
- ☐ a. found guilty.
- ☐ b. set free.
- ☐ c. laughed at.
- ☐ d. put in jail for a while.      _____

**Conclusion**    **4**    We can conclude that accidents involving cars
- ☐ a. happened most often in New York City.
- ☐ b. do not happen as often as they did in the early days of the auto.
- ☐ c. have killed many more people since Mr. Bliss was killed.
- ☐ d. were always the driver's fault.      _____

**Clarifying Devices**    **5**    The "new sets of wheels" that bicycle riders had to get used to were
- ☐ a. the new tires on their bikes.
- ☐ b. automobiles.
- ☐ c. streetcars.
- ☐ d. the bicycles themselves.      _____

**Vocabulary in Context**    **6**    Collided means
- ☐ a. hit each other hard.
- ☐ b. stopped.
- ☐ c. raced each other.
- ☐ d. traveled in the same direction.      _____

**Add your scores for questions 1–6. Enter the total here and on the graph on page 215.**    **Total Score**    _____

**11**

# 6 Sea Turtles

Did you know that a turtle can lay twelve eggs in one minute? A large sea turtle lays around 150 eggs at a time. She lays all these eggs in just a few minutes.

Large sea turtles live in the warm seas of the world. Except for when they lay their eggs, they spend their whole lives in water. When it is time to lay their eggs, the females swim to land. They usually return to the place where they themselves were born. How they find their way back there is a mystery.

When they reach shore, the big, heavy turtles crawl slowly up to the high water mark. Using their flippers, they pull themselves along the sand. They must struggle like mountain climbers to <u>attain</u> their goal. When they finally reach dry sand, they rest before beginning the difficult task of laying eggs.

The turtles lay the eggs in deep holes and cover them with warm sand. The sand protects the eggs from harm. Then the females leave them. After a few weeks, if you happened to be walking along the beach, you might see the sand begin to shake in one spot. Then you would see tiny black balls coming out of the sand. The tiny heads of baby turtles!

Baby turtles have a built-in sense of direction. As soon as they are hatched, they head for the water. Once the babies swim out to sea, they don't touch shore again until it is time for them to lay their own eggs.

| Main Idea | 1 | | |
|---|---|---|---|
| | | **Answer** | **Score** |
| | Mark the *main idea* | M | 15 |
| | Mark the statement that is *too broad* | B | 5 |
| | Mark the statement that is *too narrow* | N | 5 |

a. Sea turtles have fascinating life habits. ☐ ____

b. Sea turtles swim to shore to lay their eggs. ☐ ____

c. Large sea turtles lay their eggs in special ways. ☐ ____

**Score 15 points for each correct answer.**          Score

**Subject Matter**  2  The first sentence lets us know that this passage
   is about
   ☐ a. turtles' lives.
   ☐ b. oceans.
   ☐ c. time.
   ☐ d. the size of turtles' eggs.          _____

**Supporting Details**  3  Turtles bury their eggs
   ☐ a. to keep them cool.
   ☐ b. to protect them from danger.
   ☐ c. because of deep instinct.
   ☐ d. to protect them from the weather.          _____

**Conclusion**  4  We can conclude from this passage that
   ☐ a. many turtles die while swimming to shore.
   ☐ b. female turtles protect their babies.
   ☐ c. once turtles land, they never return to the sea.
   ☐ d. the job of laying eggs takes tremendous
       strength.          _____

**Clarifying Devices**  5  The writer compares turtles to mountain climbers
   ☐ a. because they lay their eggs in mountain areas.
   ☐ b. to give you a picture of how hard they work.
   ☐ c. to tell you that they like to climb.
   ☐ d. to tell you that mountain climbers are as
       slow as turtles.          _____

**Vocabulary in Context**  6  In this passage, the word <u>attain</u> means
   ☐ a. see.
   ☐ b. push.
   ☐ c. bury.
   ☐ d. reach.          _____

**Add your scores for questions 1–6. Enter the total here
and on the graph on page 215.**          **Total
Score**          _____

**13**

# 7 The Whale Clan

If you're looking for a whale, you have a whole family of creatures to choose from. The papa of the whale family is, of course, the whale itself. But there are other members as well. Relatives, you might say.

Few people realize that dolphins are part of the whale clan. In fact, many people do not realize that dolphins aren't fish. Fish breathe through gills and lay eggs. The dolphin does neither. Dolphins, like all the members of the whale clan, are mammals. They breathe air, and they have babies like land mammals and feed them with milk. Dolphins are fascinating to watch. They can leap high out of the water and perform turns in the air. These leaps give the dolphin time to breathe.

Porpoises also belong to the whale family and are very much like dolphins. The main difference between dolphins and porpoises is the size and shape of the snout. The dolphin's nose is long and thin. The snout of the porpoise is short and stubby. Both creatures are smart and friendly to humans.

Not all the members of the whale family are friendly. Perhaps the difference in mood has to do with size. The giant whale is much grumpier than the smaller dolphin or porpoise. An angry whale can be hard to ignore. Perhaps this <u>trait</u> helped to inspire the story of Moby Dick, the Great White Whale who sank a ship and caused the crew to drown.

| Main Idea | 1 | | |
|---|---|---|---|
| | | **Answer** | **Score** |
| | **Mark the *main idea*** | M | 15 |
| | **Mark the statement that is *too broad*** | B | 5 |
| | **Mark the statement that is *too narrow*** | N | 5 |
| | a. Like whales, dolphins are mammals. | ☐ | ___ |
| | b. An animal family is made up of many different kinds of animals. | ☐ | ___ |
| | c. Dolphins, porpoises, and whales are all part of the same family. | ☐ | ___ |

**Subject Matter**  **2**  This passage is mostly about
- ☐ a. the food whales eat.
- ☐ b. three members of the whale family.
- ☐ c. the difference between dolphins and porpoises.
- ☐ d. Moby Dick.          _____

**Supporting Details**  **3**  All members of the whale family breathe air because they are
- ☐ a. related.
- ☐ b. talented.
- ☐ c. mammals.
- ☐ d. fish.          _____

**Conclusion**  **4**  We can conclude that
- ☐ a. porpoises breathe air and feed their babies milk.
- ☐ b. porpoises are much larger than dolphins.
- ☐ c. porpoises avoid human beings.
- ☐ d. porpoises do not leap out of the water.          _____

**Clarifying Devices**  **5**  Calling porpoises and dolphins "relatives" of the whale means
- ☐ a. they are related by marriage.
- ☐ b. they belong to the same mammal family.
- ☐ c. they are born from whales.
- ☐ d. they live in the same area as whales.          _____

**Vocabulary in Context**  **6**  In this passage the word <u>trait</u> means
- ☐ a. fear.
- ☐ b. mammal.
- ☐ c. anger.
- ☐ d. characteristic.          _____

**Add your scores for questions 1–6. Enter the total here and on the graph on page 215.**

**Total Score**          _____

# 8 Give Them a Hand

Right is right. Right? Of course. But is left wrong? Well, the ancient Romans thought so. As far as they were concerned, left-handed people were mistakes of nature. Latin, the language of the Romans, had many words that expressed this view. Some words we use today still have this meaning. The Latin word *dexter* means "right." The English word *dexterous* comes from this word. It means "handy." So, right is handy. But the Latin word for "left" is *sinistra.* The English word *sinister* was derived from this word. Sinister means "evil." Is it fair to call righties handy and lefties evil? Well, fair or not, many languages have words that express similar beliefs. In Old English, the word for *left* means "weak." That isn't much of an improvement over "evil."

Not very long ago, <u>southpaws</u> were often forced to write with their right hands. Doctors have since found that this can be very harmful. You should use the hand you were born to use.

People who use their left hands are just starting to get better treatment. But why all the name calling in the first place? One reason may be that there are not as many left-handed people as there are right-handed people. People who are different are often thought to be wrong. But attitudes do seem to be changing. Fair-minded right-handed people are finally starting to give lefties a hand.

| Main Idea | 1 | | |
|---|---|---|---|
| | | **Answer** | **Score** |
| | **Mark the *main idea*** | M | 15 |
| | **Mark the statement that is *too broad*** | B | 5 |
| | **Mark the statement that is *too narrow*** | N | 5 |

a. Many languages have words that express the idea that left is bad. ☐ ____

b. Minorities often get bad treatment. ☐ ____

c. Throughout history, left-handed people have been treated poorly. ☐ ____

**Score 15 points for each correct answer.**             Score

**Subject Matter**   **2**   This passage is about
- ☐ a. Latin words.
- ☐ b. the ancient Romans.
- ☐ c. attitudes toward left-handed people.
- ☐ d. weak and evil people.

_____

**Supporting Details**   **3**   At one time, people who were left-handed were
- ☐ a. laughed at.
- ☐ b. very clumsy.
- ☐ c. forced to use their right hands.
- ☐ d. admired.

_____

**Conclusion**   **4**   Lefties today are
- ☐ a. just as weak as lefties of the past.
- ☐ b. being treated better than lefties of the past.
- ☐ c. thought to be strange.
- ☐ d. being taught to use their right hands.

_____

**Clarifying Devices**   **5**   "Fair-minded right-handed people are finally starting to give lefties a hand" means that they are
- ☐ a. applauding them.
- ☐ b. teaching them how to use their right hands.
- ☐ c. starting to give them a chance and help them out.
- ☐ d. shaking hands with them.

_____

**Vocabulary in Context**   **6**   A <u>southpaw</u> is
- ☐ a. a type of a bear.
- ☐ b. a Roman citizen.
- ☐ c. a left-handed person.
- ☐ d. a person from the South.

_____

**Add your scores for questions 1–6. Enter the total here and on the graph on page 215.**

Total
Score

_____

# 9 Six-Legged Workers

Can you imagine being able to lift fifty people at once and carry them? You'd have to have superhuman strength. Well, you may be surprised to know that tiny ants do have this kind of strength. An ant can lift a load fifty times heavier than itself! Ants must often carry food to their homes from places that are far away. To do this, they must be very strong.

Ants live in tunnels that twist and turn in many directions, like the roots of a gnarled old tree. Thousands of ants can live in one nest. The tunnels are divided into parts. Each part serves a special purpose.

The royal chamber is the place where the queen ant lays her eggs. The queen spends her whole life laying eggs. She never leaves her chamber, except to start a new nest. Worker ants must bring food to her.

The worker ants in an ant colony have many different jobs. Some workers pull the eggs from the royal chamber into a room called the "nursery." There, they help larvae climb out of their shells. Larvae are the baby ants when they first come out of the eggs. In the nursery, there are workers who look after the larvae until they become full-grown ants. Some workers look for food and store it in the granary, where seeds are kept. Others dump leftovers in the rubbish room. Ants have their own complete, busy world hidden in tunnels under our feet!

**Main Idea**      1

|  | Answer | Score |
|---|:---:|:---:|
| **Mark the *main idea*** | M | 15 |
| **Mark the statement that is *too broad*** | B | 5 |
| **Mark the statement that is *too narrow*** | N | 5 |

a. In an ant colony, the ants have many different jobs.   ☐   ____

b. Ants are very busy insects.   ☐   ____

c. An ant can carry fifty times its own weight.   ☐   ____

**Score 15 points for each correct answer.**      **Score**

**Subject Matter**    **2**    This passage is mostly about
- ☐ a. human strength.
- ☐ b. ants at work.
- ☐ c. gnarled old trees.
- ☐ d. food storage.     _____

**Supporting Details**    **3**    In the nursery, worker ants look after the
- ☐ a. queen.
- ☐ b. seeds.
- ☐ c. larvae.
- ☐ d. leftovers.     _____

**Conclusion**    **4**    Dividing the work so that each worker has a certain job helps
- ☐ a. keep the nest organized.
- ☐ b. the queen to get more food.
- ☐ c. keep the workers happy.
- ☐ d. the ants live longer.     _____

**Clarifying Devices**    **5**    The writer compares the twisting tunnels of an ant nest to
- ☐ a. the strength of humans.
- ☐ b. a gnarled old tree.
- ☐ c. a royal palace.
- ☐ d. a hospital nursery.     _____

**Vocabulary in Context**    **6**    The word gnarled means
- ☐ a. twisted.
- ☐ b. giant.
- ☐ c. confusing.
- ☐ d. difficult.     _____

**Add your scores for questions 1–6. Enter the total here and on the graph on page 215.**      **Total Score**     _____

# 10 The Collapsing Road

The young couple was very lucky. The back tires of their car stayed on the road. Otherwise, the car—and its passengers—would have fallen right into a pit twenty feet wide and thirty feet deep!

The man and woman were coming home from a party. They were enjoying the landscape around Swansea, Wales. Suddenly, they found the front of their car leaning into a huge hole. The car barely hung on to the edge of the pit. It swayed back and forth like the arm of a balance.

In their precarious position, the couple knew that each movement they made could be a matter of life and death. Slowly, slowly, they edged toward the backseat. Then each opened a back door. And on the count of three, they jumped out together. The accident was so scary that they ran a long way before they calmed down. But later they returned to see what happened. They found that a big chunk of the road had sunk into the ground! At the bottom of the pit lay their car—roof down and wheels up.

Was this mystery of the sunken road ever solved? It turned out that an abandoned mine shaft lay under the road. It had collapsed and taken the pavement with it. Layers of tunnels intersect beneath the city of Swansea. The tunnels were built so many years ago that no one knows where they end or begin. The tunnels are shaky, like those that ants build in the sand. It's even possible that the entire city might collapse.

**Main Idea** 1

| | Answer | Score |
|---|---|---|
| **Mark the *main idea*** | M | 15 |
| **Mark the statement that is *too broad*** | B | 5 |
| **Mark the statement that is *too narrow*** | N | 5 |

a. The abandoned mine tunnels below Swansea were the cause of an accident. ☐ _____

b. Swansea is a very dangerous city to drive in. ☐ _____

c. The pit in the road was very wide and deep. ☐ _____

**Score 15 points for each correct answer.**                    **Score**

**Subject Matter**     2    This passage is primarily about
☐ a. driving carefully.
☐ b. the city of Swansea, Wales.
☐ c. a road that caved in.
☐ d. tunnels that ants build.                    _____

**Supporting Details**     3    According to this selection, the pit was
☐ a. a mile wide.
☐ b. bottomless.
☐ c. part of a volcano.
☐ d. thirty feet deep.                    _____

**Conclusion**     4    It is probably true that
☐ a. the other roads in Swansea are pretty safe.
☐ b. other sections of Swansea will cave in sometime.
☐ c. everyone should move out of Swansea.
☐ d. Swansea is a very interesting city.                    _____

**Clarifying Devices**     5    The writer creates interest in the first three sentences by using
☐ a. a funny story.
☐ b. romantic imagery.
☐ c. a vivid description.
☐ d. a precise argument.                    _____

**Vocabulary in Context**     6    The word <u>precarious</u> means
☐ a. unexpected.
☐ b. dangerous.
☐ c. unusual.
☐ d. ridiculous.                    _____

**Add your scores for questions 1–6. Enter the total here and on the graph on page 215.**          **Total Score**          _____

**21**

# 11 A Whale of a Story

There has been, in history, a man who was swallowed by a whale and lived to tell the tale. The man's name was James Bartley. The records to prove his unusual experience are in the British Admiralty.

This story takes place at a time when whales were hunted for meat and oil. Bartley was making his first trip on the whaling ship *Star of the East.* Suddenly the lookout sighted a huge sperm whale. The whalers knew it was a huge whale by the size of the spray it blew into the air. They lowered their small boats. James Bartley was in the first longboat. The men rowed until they were close to the whale. A harpoon was thrown and found its mark. It sank into the whale's flesh. The maddened beast crashed into the boat, snapping its tail at the men and the wreckage of their boats. When the survivors were picked up, James Bartley was missing.

Shortly before sunset, the whale was finally captured. The sailors tied the whale's carcass to the side of the ship. Because of the hot weather it was important that they cut up the whale right away. Otherwise, the meat would begin to rot and the oil would begin to spoil. When they got to the stomach, they felt something moving about wildly. They thought it would be a big fish still alive inside. But when they opened the stomach they found James Bartley. After this trip, Bartley settled in Gloucester, England, and never returned to sea.

| Main Idea | 1 | | Answer | Score |
|---|---|---|---|---|
| | **Mark the *main idea*** | | M | 15 |
| | **Mark the statement that is *too broad*** | | B | 5 |
| | **Mark the statement that is *too narrow*** | | N | 5 |
| | a. Whaling was a dangerous business. | | ☐ | _____ |
| | b. A whale smashed a small boat from the whaling ship. | | ☐ | _____ |
| | c. James Bartley was swallowed by a whale and lived. | | ☐ | _____ |

**Score 15 points for each correct answer.**　　　**Score**

**Subject Matter**　**2**　This passage is mainly about
- ☐ a. how to hunt whales for their oil and meat.
- ☐ b. the hard and dangerous lives that whalers had to live.
- ☐ c. the duties of each man on a whaling ship.
- ☐ d. a man who managed to survive inside a whale.

　　　　　　　　　　　　　　　　　　　　　　　　　　＿＿＿

**Supporting Details**　**3**　The sailors knew that something was in the whale's stomach because
- ☐ a. they could feel something moving about wildly.
- ☐ b. the whale seemed very heavy.
- ☐ c. the whale was bulging out at one spot.
- ☐ d. the captain heard Bartley yelling for help.

　　　　　　　　　　　　　　　　　　　　　　　　　　＿＿＿

**Conclusion**　**4**　James Bartley probably never went to sea again because
- ☐ a. he wanted different kinds of adventures.
- ☐ b. of fright and shock.
- ☐ c. he was crippled by the whale.
- ☐ d. he often got seasick.

　　　　　　　　　　　　　　　　　　　　　　　　　　＿＿＿

**Clarifying Devices**　**5**　The author, in telling James Bartley's story, informs us by
- ☐ a. narrating the plain facts.
- ☐ b. referring to whaling in general.
- ☐ c. comparing whaling to other fishing.
- ☐ d. dramatically telling what happened.

　　　　　　　　　　　　　　　　　　　　　　　　　　＿＿＿

**Vocabulary in Context**　**6**　The word <u>carcass</u> refers to the
- ☐ a. whale's tail.
- ☐ b. whale's blubber.
- ☐ c. dead body of the whale.
- ☐ d. whale's side.

　　　　　　　　　　　　　　　　　　　　　　　　　　＿＿＿

**Add your scores for questions 1–6. Enter the total here and on the graph on page 215.**　　　**Total Score**　＿＿＿

# 12 The Hermit

Most people like living with other people. But some people just have to be by themselves. Take Bozo Kucik, for example. For over eighty-four years Bozo lived all alone on a desert island.

In 1888, when Bozo was only sixteen, his father left him on a little island off the coast of Croatia. He kissed Bozo goodbye and said, "I hope all goes well with you, my son." Then the father got back in his boat and sailed home without his son. How could he do such a thing, you ask? Well, Bozo had asked him to.

Bozo's father was a poor peasant who couldn't afford to feed his seven children. So he called his sons together and asked them to decide their own futures. Bozo chose the life of a <u>hermit</u>.

During the years that Bozo lived alone, World Wars I and II were fought. But Bozo never heard about them. In 1972, a crew of fishermen visited his island. They tried to talk to Bozo. At first the old hermit ran away. Finally, he let the men into his windowless stone hut.

The fishermen talked with Bozo for over two hours. They told him all about the two world wars he had missed. When they asked his age, Bozo guessed he was one hundred years old.

They asked if he wanted to go home. But Bozo said no. So the fisherman wished Bozo well and left him alone again—just as his father had eighty-four years before.

| Main Idea | 1 | | |
|---|---|---|---|
| | | **Answer** | **Score** |
| | Mark the *main idea* | M | 15 |
| | Mark the statement that is *too broad* | B | 5 |
| | Mark the statement that is *too narrow* | N | 5 |

a. Bozo lived alone on an island for eighty-four years. ☐ _____

b. Bozo was one of seven children. ☐ _____

c. Many people wish to live alone. ☐ _____

**Subject Matter**    **2**    Another good title for the passage would be
- [ ] a. Living Alone.
- [ ] b. Eighty-Four Years Alone.
- [ ] c. Why Bozo Left Home.
- [ ] d. A Desert Island.

_____

**Supporting Details**    **3**    According to the passage, Bozo's father was a
- [ ] a. fisherman.
- [ ] b. hermit.
- [ ] c. peasant.
- [ ] d. soldier.

_____

**Conclusion**    **4**    One can assume from the passage that Bozo definitely did not have which of the following?
- [ ] a. Tools
- [ ] b. Clothes
- [ ] c. Radio
- [ ] d. Food

_____

**Clarifying Devices**    **5**    When Bozo first saw the fishermen he was
- [ ] a. frightened.
- [ ] b. overjoyed.
- [ ] c. curious.
- [ ] d. angry.

_____

**Vocabulary in Context**    **6**    The best definition for the word <u>hermit</u> is someone who
- [ ] a. doesn't like people.
- [ ] b. lives on an island.
- [ ] c. lives alone.
- [ ] d. likes quiet.

_____

**Add your scores for questions 1–6. Enter the total here and on the graph on page 215.**    **Total Score**    _____

# 13 Forever Amber

Amber is a substance that lasts and lasts. Scientists are very glad of this. Without amber, we would not have many of the world's important insect remains. Amber is a hard, yellowish-brown resin found in the earth. It is translucent, which means you can see through it. It is known for its ability to preserve things.

Long ago, amber was not as hard as it is today. It was soft and gummy. Insects that weren't careful about where they walked often got trapped in it. The poor bugs that got caught in the sticky amber died. But they were forever preserved. The golden resin worked like a wax <u>mold</u>. It shaped itself around the insects. The resin hardened as the bodies of the dead insects slowly fell into decay.

The last traces of the insects trapped in amber have been gone for thousands of years. But the imprints of their bodies remained fixed in the hardened resin. Although the bugs are gone from the earth, their imprints remain for us to study. Many of these imprints are very fine and detailed. Preserved imprints of creatures and plants that once lived are called fossils. They help scientists learn more about life on earth in the past.

| Main Idea | 1 | Answer | Score |
|---|---|---|---|
| | **Mark the *main idea*** | M | 15 |
| | **Mark the statement that is *too broad*** | B | 5 |
| | **Mark the statement that is *too narrow*** | N | 5 |

a. Objects from long ago can tell us a lot about our past. ☐ _____

b. Amber has preserved the shapes of ancient insects. ☐ _____

c. Insects got caught in the sticky amber resin. ☐ _____

**Subject Matter**    **2**    This passage is about
- ☐ a. the properties of amber.
- ☐ b. how amber preserved things.
- ☐ c. how amber resin hardened.
- ☐ d. how amber was found.    _____

**Supporting Details**    **3**    Insects that walked in amber
- ☐ a. got stuck in the gooey substance.
- ☐ b. found it to be slippery.
- ☐ c. used it to build their nests.
- ☐ d. became very hard.    _____

**Conclusion**    **4**    We can conclude from this passage that amber
- ☐ a. has almost disappeared from the earth.
- ☐ b. is produced by dead insects.
- ☐ c. has played an important role in the study of prehistoric creatures.
- ☐ d. is used to make candles.    _____

**Clarifying Devices**    **5**    The gummy amber resin acted like
- ☐ a. glue.
- ☐ b. a dead insect.
- ☐ c. a wax mold.
- ☐ d. a fossil.    _____

**Vocabulary in Context**    **6**    In this case <u>mold</u> means
- ☐ a. a fungus.
- ☐ b. a form used to make a special shape.
- ☐ c. rich earth.
- ☐ d. to influence.    _____

**Add your scores for questions 1–6. Enter the total here and on the graph on page 215.**    **Total Score**    _____

# 14 Jumbo

Jumbo the elephant is one of the most famous animals that ever lived. He was the biggest elephant and the proudest possession of the British Crown.

In April of 1882, Jumbo was shipped to a zoo in the United States for a visit. He was an instant success. P. T. Barnum had heard of this giant and the great crowds he attracted. Barnum decided that he would like to have Jumbo in his circus. He thought of a way to get him.

Barnum knew that elephants in captivity have <u>periodic</u> fits of violence. He waited for Jumbo to have such a fit. When it happened, he asked the zoo to sell him the elephant. Jumbo was sold to Barnum, who paid on the spot. Jumbo became the star of the circus. Barnum made a fortune on this star.

But one day tragedy struck Jumbo. It was after a show. The elephant was being led back to his cage near the railroad tracks by his trainers. Suddenly a bright light blinded them. A train whistled, and brakes screeched as the engineer tried to stop. Dazzled by the light, Jumbo charged right into it. There was a crash that chilled the hearts of those who were there. The confused animal had run head-on into the train's engine. Jumbo died of a broken neck.

| Main Idea | 1 | | Answer | Score |
|---|---|---|---|---|
| | **Mark the *main idea*** | | M | 15 |
| | **Mark the statement that is *too broad*** | | B | 5 |
| | **Mark the statement that is *too narrow*** | | N | 5 |

a. Jumbo was dazzled by the light of a passing train. ☐ _____

b. Jumbo's long life as a circus star ended in tragedy. ☐ _____

c. Elephants are great circus attractions. ☐ _____

**Score 15 points for each correct answer.**  Score

| | | |
|---|---|---|
| **Subject Matter** | **2** | Another good title for this passage would be |

☐ a. Under the Big Top.
☐ b. P. T. Barnum's Circus.
☐ c. The Train That Killed Jumbo.
☐ d. The World's Most Famous Elephant.  _____

**Supporting Details**   **3**   P. T. Barnum

☐ a. was the head of the British zoo.
☐ b. killed Jumbo.
☐ c. stole from the British.
☐ d. bought Jumbo for his circus.  _____

**Conclusion**   **4**   Which of the following is most likely true?

☐ a. Jumbo was the biggest elephant known.
☐ b. Jumbo probably didn't die immediately after the crash.
☐ c. Jumbo could have been saved by surgery.
☐ d. Jumbo may have wanted to end his own life when he charged into the train.  _____

**Clarifying Devices**   **5**   The phrase "chilled the hearts of those who were there" means that those who saw Jumbo killed

☐ a. had no feelings.
☐ b. were fascinated.
☐ c. were shocked and upset.
☐ d. hated Jumbo.  _____

**Vocabulary in Context**   **6**   A "periodic fit of violence" is one that

☐ a. occurs every once in a while.
☐ b. happens only once.
☐ d. results in someone's death.
☐ d. is very surprising.  _____

**Add your scores for questions 1–6. Enter the total here and on the graph on page 215.**  Total Score  _____

# 15 Stunt People

They are daredevils. They are in great physical shape. They are not movie stars, but they make a lot of money. These brave folks—stunt people—are the hidden heroes of many movies.

Stunt people were around long before films. Even Shakespeare probably used them in fight scenes. To be good, a fight scene has to look real. Punches must land on enemies' jaws. Sword fights must be fought with sharp swords. Several actors are usually in a fight scene. Their moves must be set up so that no one gets hurts. It is almost like planning a dance performance.

If a movie scene is dangerous, stunt people usually fill in for the stars. You may think you see Tom Cruise running along the top of a train. But it is probably his stunt double. Stunt people must <u>resemble</u> the stars they stand in for. Their height and build should be about the same. But when close-ups are needed, the film focuses on the star.

Some stunt people specialize in certain kinds of scenes. For instance, a stunt woman named Jan Davis does all kinds of jumps. She has leapt from planes and even off the top of a waterfall. Each jump required careful planning and expert timing.

Yakima Canutt was a famous cowboy stunt man. Among other stunts, he could jump from a second story window onto a horse's back. He invented the famous trick of sliding under a moving stagecoach. (Maybe you've seen this stunt in TV westerns.) Canutt also figured out a new way to make a punch look real. He was the only stunt man ever to get an Oscar.

| Main Idea | 1 | | |
|---|---|---|---|
| | | Answer | Score |
| | Mark the *main idea* | M | 15 |
| | Mark the statement that is *too broad* | B | 5 |
| | Mark the statement that is *too narrow* | N | 5 |

a. Jan Davis and Yakima Canutt were talented stunt people. ☐ _____

b. Stunt people are brave and in good shape. ☐ _____

c. Stunt people fill in for stars in many dangerous situations ☐ _____

**Score 15 points for each correct answer.**     Score

Subject Matter    **2**    This passage is about
- ☐ a. Jan Davis.
- ☐ b. Yakima Canutt.
- ☐ c. fight scenes.
- ☐ d. the kinds of things stunt people do.

_____

Supporting Details    **3**    One trick that Yakima Canutt invented was
- ☐ a. jumping from a high window.
- ☐ b. leaping from the top of a waterfall.
- ☐ c. sliding his body under a moving stagecoach.
- ☐ d. the fight scene.

_____

Conclusion    **4**    We can conclude that Canutt won an Oscar for
- ☐ a. playing a leading man.
- ☐ b. the excellence of his stunts.
- ☐ c. being the first movie stunt man.
- ☐ d. performing in so many movies.

_____

Clarifying Devices    **5**    A well-planned fight scene is compared to a
- ☐ a. sword fight.
- ☐ b. fist fight.
- ☐ c. parachute jump.
- ☐ d. dance performance.

_____

Vocabulary in Context    **6**    The word <u>resemble</u> means
- ☐ a. look like.
- ☐ b. confuse.
- ☐ c. admire.
- ☐ d. protect.

_____

**Add your scores for questions 1–6. Enter the total here and on the graph on page 215.**     Total Score

_____

# 16 A Dragon That Flies

Although it doesn't breathe fire, this dragon can fly. And what a beauty it is. By far the scariest thing about the dragonfly is its name. This double-winged, fast-flying insect is totally harmless. It has large, deep eyes that can detect the smallest movements. Its body may be bright blue and red or a vivid green. Dragonflies in flight look like dancing spots of color in the light of a midsummer's day.

The dragonfly has a long and respectable history. It was one of the first flying insects on the earth. To see this oldster of the insect world in action, head for a pond. Dragonflies live near the water. In fact, they lay their eggs right in the water.

A dragonfly goes through several big changes before it becomes a flying insect. From the egg, a tiny creature called a nymph is hatched. It lives in the water, eating other small creatures that live in the pond. As the nymph grows, it becomes too big for its skin. Then it sheds the skin that is too small for it. Soon it grows a new one. This <u>molting</u> happens several times, until the insect is full grown. At this time it crawls up the stem of a water plant, out into the air. It squeezes its way out of its last skin as a full-fledged dragonfly.

After going through all that work to grow up, the dragonfly only lives for about a month. But for this short time it startles the hot summer air with its bright beauty.

| Main Idea | 1 | | Answer | Score |
|---|---|---|---|---|
| | | Mark the *main idea* | M | 15 |
| | | Mark the statement that is *too broad* | B | 5 |
| | | Mark the statement that is *too narrow* | N | 5 |
| | a. | Dragonflies are harmless, beautiful insects with an interesting life cycle. | ☐ | _____ |
| | b. | Dragonflies lay their eggs in the water. | ☐ | _____ |
| | c. | Insects that live near water are harmless and fascinating. | ☐ | _____ |

**Score 15 points for each correct answer.**         Score

Subject Matter   **2**   This passage is mostly about
    ☐ a. fire-breathing dragons.
    ☐ b. dragonflies
    ☐ c. pond life.
    ☐ d. flying insects                    _____

Supporting   **3**   Young dragonfly nymphs eat
Details
    ☐ a. flies.
    ☐ b. their eggs.
    ☐ c. pond vegetation.
    ☐ d. other pond creatures              _____

Conclusion   **4**   We can conclude that dragonflies are
    ☐ a. frightening to look at.
    ☐ b. good swimmers.
    ☐ c. only make-believe.
    ☐ d. ancient creatures.                _____

Clarifying   **5**   In the last sentence, the author refers to
Devices
    ☐ a. the speed of the dragonfly.
    ☐ b. the viciousness of the dragonfly.
    ☐ c. the loveliness of the dragonfly.
    ☐ d. the wings of the dragonfly.       _____

Vocabulary   **6**   <u>Molting</u> means
in Context
    ☐ a. swimming.
    ☐ b. shedding skin.
    ☐ c. growing.
    ☐ d. nymph stage.                      _____

**Add your scores for questions 1–6. Enter the total here**   Total
**and on the graph on page 215.**                             Score     _____

# 17 A Dangerous Weather Maker

Thunderstorms are dangerous because they can give off lightning. Snowstorms can tie up traffic and strand people. But tornadoes cause some of the worst weather of all.

Tornadoes are very strong columns of twisting air. They come out of rain clouds and form funnels. The funnels move along the ground, picking up anything in their path. Tornado winds can be over 300 miles an hour. Property damage can be terrible.

Most of the world's tornadoes are in the United States. The flat middle section of the country—the Great Plains—is where many strike. Spring is the most common time for tornadoes. But they hit in other seasons, too.

Tornadoes can be rated by the damage that their winds do. The worst tornadoes have winds between 261 and 318 miles an hour. They can lift a sturdy wooden house off its <u>foundation</u>. They can even carry cars through the air. Luckily, tornadoes this strong don't happen very often.

The world's worst tornado happened in March 1925. It went through three states—Missouri, Illinois, and Indiana. It killed about seven hundred people and injured over two thousand. In one small town, over two hundred people were killed. Many of the dead were school children.

If you hear that a tornado is coming, look for a safe place right away. If you are indoors, go to a basement. If you are outside, lie flat on the ground. Treat these storms with respect.

**Main Idea**    1

|  | Answer | Score |
|---|---|---|
| Mark the *main idea* | M | 15 |
| Mark the statement that is *too broad* | B | 5 |
| Mark the statement that is *too narrow* | N | 5 |

a. Tornadoes are storms that cause very severe damage in the United States. ☐ _____

b. Some tornadoes have winds over 300 miles an hour. ☐ _____

c. Many kinds of weather can cause problems. ☐ _____

**Score 15 points for each correct answer.**                    Score

**Subject Matter**    2    This passage is about
    ☐ a. what tornadoes are and what they do.
    ☐ b. the world's worst tornado.
    ☐ c. the rules of tornado safety.
    ☐ d. why tornadoes are different than thunderstorms and snowstorms.                    _____

**Supporting Details**    3    The world's worst tornado cut across
    ☐ a. the southern United States.
    ☐ b. the Great Plains.
    ☐ c. Missouri, Illinois, and Indiana.
    ☐ d. a funnel.                    _____

**Conclusion**    4    Because many children were killed in the world's worst tornado, we can conclude that
    ☐ a. the tornado happened at night.
    ☐ b. the tornado must have hit one or more schools.
    ☐ c. children think tornadoes are funny.
    ☐ d. no adults were killed.                    _____

**Clarifying Devices**    5    The sentence "Treat these storms with respect" means
    ☐ a. tell other people about them.
    ☐ b. read more about the damage they can cause.
    ☐ c. take them seriously.
    ☐ d. be sure your house has a basement.                    _____

**Vocabulary in Context**    6    Foundation means
    ☐ a. a very hard rock.
    ☐ b. the base of a building.
    ☐ c. a large company.
    ☐ d. a city-sized lot.                    _____

**Add your scores for questions 1–6. Enter the total here and on the graph on page 215.**          Total Score          _____

# 18 Oldest, Youngest, or in the Middle?

Were you the first or last child in your family? Or were you a middle or only child? Some people think it matters where you were born in your family. But there are different ideas about what birth order means.

Some people say that oldest children are smart and strong-willed. They are very likely to be successful. The reason for this is simple. Parents have a lot of time for their first child. They give him or her a lot of attention. So this child is very likely to do well. An only child will succeed for the same reason.

What happens to the other children in a family? Middle children don't get so much attention. So they don't feel that important. If a family has many children, the middle ones sometimes get lost in the crowd. The youngest child, though, often gets special treatment. He or she is the "baby." Often this child grows up to be funny and charming.

Do you believe these ideas about birth order? A recent study saw things quite differently. This study found that first children believed in family rules. They didn't take many chances in their lives. They usually followed orders. Rules didn't mean so much to later children in a family. They went out and followed their own ideas. They took chances. And they often did better in life.

Which <u>theory</u> about birth order do you believe? Look at your own family or your friends' families. Decide which idea fits what you see.

**Main Idea**    1 —————————————————————————————

| | Answer | Score |
|---|---|---|
| **Mark the *main idea*** | M | 15 |
| **Mark the statement that is *too broad*** | B | 5 |
| **Mark the statement that is *too narrow*** | N | 5 |

a. There are two different ideas about the meaning of birth order. ☐ _____

b. First children grow up to be like only children. ☐ _____

c. Birth order matters in people's lives. ☐ _____

**Score 15 points for each correct answer.**   **Score**

**Subject Matter**   **2**   This passage is about
☐ a. why the oldest children in a family usually succeed.
☐ b. why some children refuse to follow orders.
☐ c. ways in which birth order may affect how children grow up.
☐ d. how people have a lot of trouble agreeing about ideas.

_____

**Supporting Details**   **3**   According to the article, some people think that youngest children grow up to be
☐ a. babies.
☐ b. not capable of doing anything.
☐ c. funny and charming.
☐ d. strong leaders.

_____

**Conclusion**   **4**   If later-born children take chances rather than following rules, you might expect them to be
☐ a. jealous.
☐ b. creative.
☐ c. spoiled.
☐ d. obedient employees.

_____

**Clarifying Devices**   **5**   The statement that middle children "sometimes get lost in the crowd" means that
☐ a. they have a poor sense of direction.
☐ b. they don't get a lot of attention.
☐ c. they have a strong desire to be leaders.
☐ d. they can't get along with others.

_____

**Vocabulary in Context**   **6**   The word <u>theory</u> means
☐ a. idea.
☐ b. comparison.
☐ c. evidence.
☐ d. surprise.

_____

**Add your scores for questions 1–6. Enter the total here and on the graph on page 215.**   **Total Score**

_____

# 19 A Very Old Riddle

The people of old Greece and Egypt believed in <u>mythology</u>. The stories in myths were mostly about strange creatures. Some of these creatures were part human and part animal. One, the Sphinx, had the head of a woman and the body of a lion. The Sphinx lived high on a mountain peak over which a road passed.

People who traveled that road were never heard from again. Whenever travelers reached the peak of the mountain, the Sphinx would block the road and speak this riddle: "What goes on four feet in the morning, on two feet at noon, and on three feet in the evening?" No traveler in a thousand years had guessed the answer. And the Sphinx had eaten them all.

But one day a Greek traveler named Oedipus traveled that way. When Oedipus came to the mountain pass, the Sphinx leaped out. With a catlike grin, it asked its terrible riddle. Oedipus, wise with age, knew the answer immediately, but he teased the Sphinx by frowning and shaking his head. These strange actions made the Sphinx tense and upset. Then suddenly Oedipus shot forth the answer. The Sphinx was so upset that it jumped off the mountain to its death.

The answer Oedipus gave was simple: a person. Can you guess why this was right? In a person's morning, or childhood, he or she crawls on all fours. At noon, as an adult, a person walks on two legs. In the evening, old age, a person uses a third foot—a cane.

**Main Idea**　1

| | Answer | Score |
|---|---|---|
| Mark the *main idea* | M | 15 |
| Mark the statement that is *too broad* | B | 5 |
| Mark the statement that is *too narrow* | N | 5 |

a. The Sphinx asked a riddle that only Oedipus could answer. ☐ _____

b. Greek and Egyptian myths contain stories of many strange creatures. ☐ _____

c. The Sphinx asked a difficult riddle of all travelers who passed by. ☐ _____

**Score 15 points for each correct answer.** Score

**Subject Matter**    **2**    Another good title for this passage would be
- ☐ a. The History of Greece.
- ☐ b. The Sphinx and Its Riddle.
- ☐ c. Mythical Beasts of Greece and Egypt.
- ☐ d. Oedipus and His Riddle.

_____

**Supporting Details**    **3**    The Sphinx was
- ☐ a. half man and half woman.
- ☐ b. half woman and half camel.
- ☐ c. half woman and half lion.
- ☐ d. half lion and half horse.

_____

**Conclusion**    **4**    The writer suggests that Oedipus was the first to
- ☐ a. see the Sphinx.
- ☐ b. answer the riddle correctly.
- ☐ c. defeat the mighty Sphinx in battle.
- ☐ d. try to answer the riddle.

_____

**Clarifying Devices**    **5**    In the Sphinx's riddle, morning, noon, and evening
- ☐ a. symbolize different parts of life.
- ☐ b. have no meaning.
- ☐ c. are used to mean different times of day.
- ☐ d. are the answers to the riddle.

_____

**Vocabulary in Context**    **6**    <u>Mythology</u> deals with stories that are
- ☐ a. true.
- ☐ b. historical.
- ☐ c. legends.
- ☐ d. for children.

_____

**Add your scores for questions 1–6. Enter the total here and on the graph on page 215.**    Total Score _____

# 20 Protect Your Hearing

Is your roommate's stereo playing too loud? Is the neighbor's leaf blower driving you crazy? The world seems to be getting noisier all the time. And you need to be concerned about it. All those loud sounds may actually damage your ears.

Noise can affect your hearing in two ways. A very loud noise very close to the ear can injure it right away. An example might be the sound from a high-powered rifle. A loud blast like this can leave scars on your inner ear tissues. You will hear less well as a result. (That is why people at shooting ranges wear coverings to protect their ears.)

Much hearing damage comes more slowly. It occurs over a period of time. You have probably heard of people in rock bands who lose their hearing. The constant loud noise gradually damages their ears. But this can happen to other people as well. Loud noise comes from fireworks, from car horns in traffic, even from vacuum cleaners. Too much of any of these can affect your hearing.

How can people protect their ears? One way is to use earplugs. Is the concert so loud that you can't hear what your friend is saying? Put the plugs in. And sometimes give your ears a rest. Go to that noisy basketball game tonight. But don't run your lawn mower tomorrow morning.

As people grow older, their hearing skills gradually decrease. This is a fairly natural <u>phenomenon</u>. But hearing loss by age thirty is not natural. You can avoid it if you are careful.

## Main Idea 1

|  | Answer | Score |
|---|---|---|
| Mark the *main idea* | M | 15 |
| Mark the statement that is *too broad* | B | 5 |
| Mark the statement that is *too narrow* | N | 5 |

a. Various kinds of loud noise can cause ear damage. ☐ _____

b. It's a noisy world out there. ☐ _____

c. Always use protective ear coverings at a shooting range. ☐ _____

**Score 15 points for each correct answer.**

**Subject Matter**    2    This passage is mostly about
    ☐ a. stereos and leaf blowers.
    ☐ b. using earplugs to protect your hearing.
    ☐ c. hearing loss by age thirty.
    ☐ d. the kinds of noises that can damage your ears.    _____

**Supporting Details**    3    Two basic ways that hearing loss can occur are
    ☐ a. suddenly and gradually.
    ☐ b. from guns and from vacuum cleaners.
    ☐ c. from childhood noises and from bad practices as an adult.
    ☐ d. from childhood noises and from natural hearing loss in old age.    _____

**Conclusion**    4    Typical seventy-five-year-old people can expect their hearing to be
    ☐ a. excellent.
    ☐ b. terrible.
    ☐ c. not quite as good as when they were younger.
    ☐ d. able to be improved through surgery.    _____

**Clarifying Devices**    5    The result of scars forming on your inner ear tissues is that you
    ☐ a. will hear less well.
    ☐ b. will hear ringing in your ears for a few weeks.
    ☐ c. can shoot a rifle without the noise affecting you.
    ☐ d. should avoid listening to rock music.    _____

**Vocabulary in Context**    6    A phenomenon is
    ☐ a. a loud noise.
    ☐ b. a fact or event that can be observed.
    ☐ d. a specific viewpoint.
    ☐ d. a statement requiring proof.    _____

**Add your scores for questions 1–6. Enter the total here and on the graph on page 215.**    Total Score    _____

# 21 The Wizard of Wall Street

At the age of eighty, Hetty Green lived like a <u>pauper</u> in an unheated apartment. To save the cost of heating her food, she ate only cold eggs and onions. In order to save more money, Hetty wore newspapers instead of underwear. She had only the bottoms of her dresses cleaned. A very poor person, you say? No, Hetty was one of America's richest women!

Hetty Green was born in 1835 in a rich section of Bellow Falls, Vermont. When her father died, she was left a large fortune. She took all of her money and invested it in the stock market. Her stocks did so well that she became known as "the wizard of Wall Street."

But though she was very rich, Hetty Green was extremely cheap. For instance, when her son, Edward, broke his leg, she refused to call for a doctor. She felt it would cost too much. So she carried her son to a charity hospital. Still, young Edward's leg got worse. Finally, the leg had to be removed to save the boy's life. But Hetty still didn't want to pay the hospital fee. Instead, in order to save more money, she had her son's operation done on the kitchen table in her rooming house.

When Hetty died in 1916, she was worth over $120 million. Yet this tight-fisted woman had lived as though she barely had a cent.

| Main Idea | 1 | | | |
|---|---|---|---|---|
| | | | Answer | Score |
| | **Mark the *main idea*** | | M | 15 |
| | **Mark the statement that is *too broad*** | | B | 5 |
| | **Mark the statement that is *too narrow*** | | N | 5 |
| | a. Hetty Green was rich, but she lived like a poor person. | | ☐ | ____ |
| | b. Hetty Green ate only cold food. | | ☐ | ____ |
| | c. Hetty Green was an unusual person. | | ☐ | ____ |

**Score 15 points for each correct answer.**       Score

**Subject Matter**    2    Another good title for this story might be
- [ ] a. How to Make a Million Dollars.
- [ ] b. The Cheap Millionaire.
- [ ] c. Poor Hetty Green.
- [ ] d. Cheap Medical Care.

_____

**Supporting Details**    3    Hetty carried her son to a charity hospital because
- [ ] a. she had no money.
- [ ] b. her son refused to see a doctor.
- [ ] c. the doctor refused to come to her house.
- [ ] d. she refused to call for a doctor.

_____

**Conclusion**    4    It is obvious from the passage that Hetty was
- [ ] a. very poor as a child.
- [ ] b. a very good businesswoman.
- [ ] c. afraid of doctors.
- [ ] d. poor in her old age.

_____

**Clarifying Devices**    5    The author tells us about Hetty's son's accident
- [ ] a. to show us that she was a good mother.
- [ ] b. to show us how she felt about doctors.
- [ ] c. to show us how brave Edward was.
- [ ] d. to show us just how cheap she was.

_____

**Vocabulary in Context**    6    What is the best definition for the word <u>pauper</u>?
- [ ] a. Greedy person
- [ ] b. Old person
- [ ] c. Poor person
- [ ] d. Cheap person

_____

**Add your scores for questions 1–6. Enter the total here and on the graph on page 216.**    Total Score    _____

# 22  Surviving in Very Cold Climates

Imagine going to sleep in October and waking up in May! Animals such as marmots and ground squirrels stay warm by sleeping all winter. All this time, they do not wake up once. This special kind of sleep is called hibernation. During this sleep, the heart slows down, and the animal breathes more slowly. It doesn't move around, so it uses less energy.

Animals like the marmot and the ground squirrel <u>inhabit</u> the coldest parts of the world. They need special talents to survive in these frigid places. Their furry coats keep them snug when the temperature falls below zero. It often gets this cold in the Arctic, a land that is just below the North Pole.

Before the long winter, some animals eat and eat. After a while, they grow very fat. When winter comes, they live on the fat saved up in their bodies. The fat layers help keep them warm.

Arctic animals also have other ways to beat the cold. Rabbits in the Arctic, for example, have very small ears. Small ears keep heat in, while big ears let it out. Small things usually keep heat in. Have you ever slept in a room that is very small and noticed how hot it can get?

It rarely gets warm in the Arctic. But although summer seasons there are very short, the sun shines brightly. Plants seem to spring up before your eyes! Animals such as caribou look forward all year to summer, when they can eat fresh grass again. Every minute of sunshine is important to their lives.

**Main Idea**   1

|  | Answer | Score |
|---|---|---|
| **Mark the *main idea*** | M | 15 |
| **Mark the statement that is *too broad*** | B | 5 |
| **Mark the statement that is *too narrow*** | N | 5 |

a. Some animals live in cold parts of the globe.  ☐  _____

b. Arctic animals have many ways of keeping out the cold.  ☐  _____

c. Some Arctic animals hibernate.  ☐  _____

**Score 15 points for each correct answer.**  **Score**

**Subject Matter**  2  Another good title for this passage would be
- ☐ a. The Arctic Summer.
- ☐ b. Marmots and Squirrels.
- ☐ c. Keeping Warm in the Arctic.
- ☐ d. Freezing Temperatures.

_____

**Supporting Details**  3  The Arctic is a land
- ☐ a. near the equator.
- ☐ b. near the South Pole.
- ☐ c. without any sunlight.
- ☐ d. just below the North Pole.

_____

**Conclusion**  4  After reading this passage, we can guess that when an animal moves around, it
- ☐ a. is very restless.
- ☐ b. uses more energy.
- ☐ c. is looking for food.
- ☐ d. has lost its young.

_____

**Clarifying Devices**  5  To help the reader understand that small things keep heat in, the writer uses
- ☐ a. an example.
- ☐ b. a strong argument.
- ☐ c. scientific facts.
- ☐ d. careful measurements.

_____

**Vocabulary in Context**  6  Inhabit means
- ☐ a. roam.
- ☐ b. survive.
- ☐ c. live in.
- ☐ d. fear.

_____

**Add your scores for questions 1–6. Enter the total here and on the graph on page 216.**  **Total Score**

_____

# 23 Let's Shake on It

What could be simpler than shaking fruit from a tree? Well, the job is a lot tougher than you might think. There is definitely a right way and a wrong way to shake a fruit tree. And a person who is a good apple tree shaker may not be a good cherry tree shaker. Different fruits take different shakes.

As a rule, a slow, hard shake is best. This makes the fruit fall much faster than a light, quick jiggle. Most fruits have a <u>set</u> number of shakes per minute that will do the best job of getting them out of the tree and onto the ground. To shake down plums, try shaking the tree four hundred times per minute, moving the tree two inches at each shake. Experts say you'll get three times more fruit from the tree than you will if you shake eleven hundred times per minute at one inch per shake. Cherries, because they are smaller, need more jarring. A good rate of shaking seems to be about twelve hundred shakes per minute. Apples, like plums, need about four hundred shakes.

Of course, some folks may choose to ignore all these expert directions for jiggling fruit. Can you actually imagine shaking a tree so many times? Besides, keeping track of all the numbers can be enough to drive some people up a tree.

| Main Idea | 1 | Answer | Score |
|---|---|---|---|
| **Mark the *main idea*** | | M | 15 |
| **Mark the statement that is *too broad*** | | B | 5 |
| **Mark the statement that is *too narrow*** | | N | 5 |

| | | |
|---|---|---|
| a. Some tasks are more complicated than they look. | ☐ | _____ |
| b. Shaking fruit trees can be a real art. | ☐ | _____ |
| c. Different fruits require different amounts of shaking. | ☐ | _____ |

**Subject Matter**  2  This passage is concerned with
- [ ] a. eating plums.
- [ ] b. how to shake fruit from a tree.
- [ ] c. the value of fruits and vegetables.
- [ ] d. ways in which people shake.

_____

**Supporting Details**  3  A smaller fruit normally requires
- [ ] a. a ladder.
- [ ] b. less shaking.
- [ ] c. two people per tree.
- [ ] d. more shaking.

_____

**Conclusion**  4  From this passage we can conclude that
- [ ] a. good fruit pickers know how fast or slow to shake a tree.
- [ ] b. most of the fruits are badly bruised when they hit the ground.
- [ ] c. it really makes no difference how you shake a fruit tree.
- [ ] d. too much shaking can damage the branches.

_____

**Clarifying Devices**  5  The writer ends this story with
- [ ] a. a serious thought.
- [ ] b. a suggestion for other ways to get fruit from trees.
- [ ] c. a joke.
- [ ] d. a warning.

_____

**Vocabulary in Context**  6  The word <u>set</u> means
- [ ] a. tiresome.
- [ ] b. great.
- [ ] c. fixed.
- [ ] d. collected.

_____

**Add your scores for questions 1–6. Enter the total here and on the graph on page 216.**  Total Score

_____

# 24 Slow but Sure

Nowadays the Indianapolis 500, one of the world's most famous car races, takes about three-and-a-half hours to run. If the Indy 500 had been held in 1895, it would have taken almost three days. The horseless carriage had just been invented a short time before. Top speeds back then were much lower than they are today. For most people, just seeing a car move without a horse pulling it was thrilling enough. The driver's main concern was making sure the car didn't break down.

One of the first car races was held in Chicago on Thanksgiving Day in 1895. Folks crowded the streets to <u>gawk</u> at the new machines. The route of the race went through the heart of town. The cars were to go out to a nearby suburb and back. The race covered a distance of about fifty-four miles. That's less than one-tenth the distance at Indy. The drivers cranked up their engines and prayed that they wouldn't conk out. Then they were off. The race proved too much for some of the cars. Perhaps they couldn't withstand the high speeds. The winner of the contest was J. Frank Duryea. He got the checkered flag a bit more than seven hours after he started. He had covered the grueling distance at an average speed of 7.5 miles per hour. That is slower than a modern marathoner can go on foot. Even so, as Duryea finished, the crowd went wild.

| Main Idea | 1 | | Answer | Score |
|---|---|---|---|---|
| | **Mark the *main idea*** | | M | 15 |
| | **Mark the statement that is *too broad*** | | B | 5 |
| | **Mark the statement that is *too narrow*** | | N | 5 |
| | a. Things don't have to be done quickly to be done well. | | ☐ | _____ |
| | b. Early auto races were very slow compared with today's races. | | ☐ | _____ |
| | c. One of the first auto races was held in Chicago. | | ☐ | _____ |

**Subject Matter**    **2**    This passage deals with
- [ ] a. the Indianapolis 500.
- [ ] b. a new kind of car.
- [ ] c. an early auto race.
- [ ] d. the streets of Chicago.

**Supporting Details**    **3**    Some cars didn't finish the race in Chicago because
- [ ] a. their engines broke down.
- [ ] b. the drivers were afraid of the high speeds.
- [ ] c. the brakes jammed.
- [ ] d. they ran out of gas.

**Conclusion**    **4**    What can you conclude about the public's attitude toward auto races?
- [ ] a. They were more impressed with slower speeds.
- [ ] b. They thought cars were unnecessary.
- [ ] c. They enjoyed just seeing the cars.
- [ ] d. They were easily bored.

**Clarifying Devices**    **5**    This passage is mainly
- [ ] a. a description of an event.
- [ ] b. a set of historical facts.
- [ ] c. a list of racing statistics
- [ ] d. a biography of an auto racer.

**Vocabulary in Context**    **6**    In this passage the word <u>gawk</u> means
- [ ] a. laugh.
- [ ] b. stare.
- [ ] c. frown.
- [ ] d. glare.

**Add your scores for questions 1–6. Enter the total here and on the graph on page 216.**    **Total Score**    _____

# 25 Scallops and Clams

Scallops and clams are both mollusks—shelled sea creatures with soft bodies. Yet they have more differences than similarities. Scallops and clams both feed by pulling water through their shells and straining out tiny plants and animals as their food. Both shellfish are popular prey for many other sea creatures. But when it comes to searching for safety, they have very different ways.

The scallop lies on the floor of the ocean in shallow to fairly deep water. Its curved shell raises it just above the sand or gravel on the bottom. It looks almost helpless lying there. But don't let it fool you. There is a ring of tiny eyes peering out from the scallop's shell. At the first sign of an enemy, the scallop takes off, swimming by jetting spurts of water out behind it. It's a very fast swimmer.

Any clam that dared to lie in full view on the ocean floor would quickly be eaten. Clams make a tasty meal for starfish, crabs, or carnivorous snails. They move very slowly and cannot swim at all. They find safety by burrowing deep into the mud or sand. Their long necks stretch like periscopes, up to the top of the sand. Just the tip of the neck pokes out to get food for the clam. If anything comes near, the neck can quickly be pulled back within the shell. The clam stays safe below the surface, two or three feet down.

| Main Idea | 1 | | |
|---|---|---|---|
| | | **Answer** | **Score** |
| | Mark the *main idea* | M | 15 |
| | Mark the statement that is *too broad* | B | 5 |
| | Mark the statement that is *too narrow* | N | 5 |

a. Scallops and clams live on the ocean floor. ☐ _____

b. Scallops and clams use different methods to defend themselves. ☐ _____

c. Scallops and clams are good prey for many other ocean creatures. ☐ _____

**Subject Matter**    **2**    This passage focuses on
- ☐ a. predators of clams and scallops.
- ☐ b. how scallops and clams protect themselves.
- ☐ c. the similarities between scallops and clams.
- ☐ d. how scallops and clams feed.     _____

**Supporting Details**    **3**    Clams and scallops eat
- ☐ a. fish.
- ☐ b. crabs.
- ☐ c. tiny plants and animals.
- ☐ d. water.     _____

**Conclusion**    **4**    Based on this passage, which statement is most likely to be true?
- ☐ a. Scallops are smarter than clams.
- ☐ b. A clam has no need for eyes.
- ☐ c. Scallops have longer necks than clams.
- ☐ d. Clams are more cowardly than scallops.     _____

**Clarifying Devices**    **5**    The writer compares a clam's neck to
- ☐ a. a giraffe's neck.
- ☐ b. a skyscraper.
- ☐ c. a snorkel.
- ☐ d. a periscope.     _____

**Vocabulary in Context**    **6**    <u>Jetting</u> means
- ☐ a. squirting.
- ☐ b. exploding.
- ☐ c. flying.
- ☐ d. leaving.     _____

**Add your scores for questions 1–6. Enter the total here and on the graph on page 216.**     **Total Score**     _____

# 26 Joker's Wild

Watch out for practical jokers. They'll do almost anything for a laugh. One such prankster was Moe Drabowsky. He was a baseball relief pitcher. Relief pitchers are standby players who replace the starting pitcher in a game if he is pitching badly. If the starting pitcher is throwing well, relief pitchers have nothing to do. They just sit around in the bullpen and hope the manager calls them to play.

Waiting around in the bullpen gave Moe lots of time to think up jokes. But his best joke was played after he retired from baseball. Moe was sitting at home watching his team play on television. It would have been a boring game for him had he still been on the team. The starting pitcher was doing great. He hadn't given up a single run. The relief pitchers wouldn't be likely to play in this game. The last thing they'd expect would be a call from the manager. The thought gave Moe a mischievous idea. He still remembered the bullpen phone number. Moe dialed it from his living room. A startled relief pitcher answered. Using a voice that sounded like the manager's, Moe growled, "Warm up and get ready to play." The star pitcher gaped at the man in the bullpen who was getting ready to pitch. Everyone stared at the manager in disbelief. The poor manager could only scratch his head. A thousand miles away, Moe Drabowsky sat in his living room watching the event on TV and laughing.

| Main Idea | 1 | Answer | Score |
|---|---|---|---|
| | **Mark the *main idea*** | M | 15 |
| | **Mark the statement that is *too broad*** | B | 5 |
| | **Mark the statement that is *too narrow*** | N | 5 |

a. Moe Drabowsky played a great practical joke on his team after he retired from baseball. ☐ _____

b. Moe Drabowsky could make his voice sound like the team manager's. ☐ _____

c. Moe Drabowsky played a lot of practical jokes. ☐ _____

52

**Score 15 points for each correct answer.**                    **Score**

**Subject Matter**     **2**   This passage is concerned with
          ☐ a. a baseball game.
          ☐ b. a practical joke.
          ☐ c. advice on pitching.
          ☐ d. a TV show.           \_\_\_\_\_

**Supporting Details**     **3**   The relief pitcher who answered the phone in the bullpen thought he was talking to
          ☐ a. the President.
          ☐ b. his manager.
          ☐ c. Moe.
          ☐ d. the phone company.         \_\_\_\_\_

**Conclusion**     **4**   We can assume that Moe made the call
          ☐ a. because he was jealous of the successful pitchers.
          ☐ b. from a phone booth.
          ☐ c. long distance.
          ☐ d. during the winter.         \_\_\_\_\_

**Clarifying Devices**     **5**   This passage
          ☐ a. makes fun of baseball players.
          ☐ b. tells you how to play practical jokes on people.
          ☐ c. teaches a lesson.
          ☐ d. tells an amusing story.         \_\_\_\_\_

**Vocabulary in Context**     **6**   In this passage the word <u>gaped</u> means
          ☐ a. yelled.
          ☐ b. glanced.
          ☐ c. stared with open mouth.
          ☐ d. waved.         \_\_\_\_\_

**Add your scores for questions 1–6. Enter the total here and on the graph on page 216.**      **Total Score**      \_\_\_\_\_

# 27  The Mysterious Iceman

Put yourself in these tourists' position. You are walking an icy mountain path in the Alps in Europe. Suddenly you <u>spot</u> a body on the ground, face downward and stuck to the ice. You think someone may have been murdered or in a fatal accident. So you rush back and call the police. The police, however, quickly realize that this body is different from others they've found on the mountain. For one thing, it is mostly undamaged. For another, its skin is dried out, like a mummy's. And with it is a knife with a small stone blade.

The body turned out to be much older than the tourists could have guessed. When specialists had a chance to examine it, they discovered it had been there for about five thousand years!

How could a body stay preserved for all this time? Two things probably helped. First, the place where the man died was somewhat sheltered, so animals couldn't get at it. Then he was quickly covered by falling snow. Wind blowing through the snow probably "freeze-dried" his body, removing all moisture from it.

Objects found with the body told something about the Iceman's life. He wore a well-made fur jacket and pants. He clearly had been hunting, for he carried arrows, and animal bones were nearby. He also had a braided grass mat for sitting or sleeping on. Perhaps he was exhausted when he lay down for the last time.

The body was found in 1991, when some of the ice on the mountain melted. Searching for the cause of the Iceman's death, scientists put the body back into cold conditions—and hoped.

| Main Idea | 1 | Answer | Score |
|---|---|---|---|
| | **Mark the *main idea*** | **M** | 15 |
| | **Mark the statement that is *too broad*** | **B** | 5 |
| | **Mark the statement that is *too narrow*** | **N** | 5 |

a. The life and death of the Iceman is a puzzle for scientists. ☐ _____

b. Bodies over five thousand years old are extremely rare. ☐ _____

c. The body was very well preserved. ☐ _____

**Subject Matter**    **2**    Another title for this passage might be

     ☐ a. The Amazing Find on the Mountain.

     ☐ b. What Life Was Like Five Thousand Years Ago.

     ☐ c. The Frightened Tourists.

     ☐ d. The Clothes of the Iceman.       _____

**Supporting**    **3**    The man died in a location that was
**Details**

     ☐ a. near the base of the mountain.

     ☐ b. sheltered.

     ☐ c. surrounded by open fields.

     ☐ d. cold and isolated.       _____

**Conclusion**    **4**    The time of the year that the Iceman died was probably

     ☐ a. early fall.

     ☐ b. late spring.

     ☐ c. summer.

     ☐ d. winter.       _____

**Clarifying**    **5**    To explain why the police realized this body
**Devices**          was "different," the passage gives

     ☐ a. the tourists' story.

     ☐ b. three reasons.

     ☐ c. a detailed description of the death site.

     ☐ d. a scientist's opinion.       _____

**Vocabulary**    **6**    In this passage the word <u>spot</u> means
**in Context**

     ☐ a. a tiny dot.

     ☐ b. an exact location.

     ☐ c. see.

     ☐ d. ignore.       _____

**Add your scores for questions 1–6. Enter the total here**    **Total**
**and on the graph on page 216.**                           **Score**       _____

# 28 They'll Eat Anything

You know that pearls grow inside oysters, but would you ever think to look for diamonds inside an ostrich? Well, a hunter once shot an ostrich and discovered, to his great surprise, that the big bird had swallowed a bunch of diamonds. How could such a strange thing happen?

Like many other birds, the ostrich swallows small stones that stay inside its "gizzard." The gizzard is a bird's second stomach. It is where the food is ground up. The small stones help to grind up the food so it can be digested. The small stones do the chewing, because birds don't have teeth. In the case of the ostrich with the diamonds, the bird simply had expensive taste in rocks. He used the diamonds to help digest his dinner.

Diamonds and stones aren't all that an ostrich will swallow. If there are no stones around, it will eat just about anything. Sadly for ostriches in zoos, this can be a <u>fatal</u> habit. The tendency to swallow anything it sees has caused the death of many an ostrich. Cruel or careless people often throw things into the bird's living space. They throw keys, coins, and even large objects such as horseshoes. The ostrich swallows them without hesitation. Coins can be the worst. Inside the ostrich they wear down to a razor-sharp edge. They will cut open the bird's gizzard from the inside. When one young zoo ostrich died, 484 coins weighing more than eight pounds were found in its gizzard.

| Main Idea | 1 | | |
|---|---|---|---|
| | | **Answer** | **Score** |
| | **Mark the *main idea*** | M | 15 |
| | **Mark the statement that is *too broad*** | B | 5 |
| | **Mark the statement that is *too narrow*** | N | 5 |
| | a. Birds often eat strange things. | ☐ | _____ |
| | b. Ostriches will swallow anything to help them digest food. | ☐ | _____ |
| | c. One ostrich died with 484 coins in its gizzard. | ☐ | _____ |

**Subject Matter**  2  This passage is about
- ☐ a. ostriches.
- ☐ b. diamonds.
- ☐ c. people at the zoo.
- ☐ d. rock hunting.     _____

**Supporting Details**  3  Ostriches eat stones because they don't have
- ☐ a. enough food.
- ☐ b. bird seed.
- ☐ c. teeth.
- ☐ d. diamonds.     _____

**Conclusion**  4  The ostrich is not smart enough to
- ☐ a. digest its own food.
- ☐ b. eat only diamonds.
- ☐ c. avoid eating objects that are harmful.
- ☐ d. escape from the zoo.     _____

**Clarifying Devices**  5  The phrase "The small stones do the chewing" makes rocks seem as though they are
- ☐ a. important.
- ☐ b. alive.
- ☐ c. dangerous.
- ☐ d. uncomfortable.     _____

**Vocabulary in Context**  6  Fatal is another word for
- ☐ a. foolish.
- ☐ b. careless.
- ☐ c. deadly.
- ☐ d. cruel.     _____

**Add your scores for questions 1–6. Enter the total here and on the graph on page 216.**     Total Score     _____

# 29 No Laughing Matter

Never laugh at a snow-covered mountain! Laughter and yelling during the avalanche season can trigger a deadly pile of snow. Huge snow slides are most common in mountains where there are steep slopes that are well buried in snow and ice. The snow builds up slowly and lands very softly. This can create a very touchy, <u>unstable</u> situation. Tons of snow may be held up by only the friction between snowflakes. The deep snow is like a house of cards. The slightest movement can cause it to tumble. As soon as something slips, a great mass of snow will come crashing down the mountainside.

Slides may be started by sound vibrations. They may also be started by the weight of wet, melting snow. Once an avalanche has been triggered, the cause no longer matters. Moving down a steep slope, it picks up great speed and added snow. Some avalanches travel as fast as 200 miles per hour. The force of an avalanche will mow down anything in its path. Whole houses have been swallowed up by these fast-paced piles of snow.

The wind that is caused by an avalanche is almost as destructive as the snow itself. Winds from an avalanche have been known to travel as fast as those of a tornado. So, when approaching a thickly snow-covered mountain, speak softly!

| Main Idea | 1 | | Answer | Score |
|-----------|---|---|--------|-------|
| | **Mark the *main idea*** | | M | 15 |
| | **Mark the statement that is *too broad*** | | B | 5 |
| | **Mark the statement that is *too narrow*** | | N | 5 |

| | | Answer | Score |
|---|---|--------|-------|
| a. | Mountain areas can be very dangerous. | ☐ | _____ |
| b. | Sound vibrations can trigger an avalanche. | ☐ | _____ |
| c. | Avalanches, which are huge piles of tumbling snow, are very dangerous. | ☐ | _____ |

**Score 15 points for each correct answer.**          **Score**

**Subject Matter**  **2**  This passage is concerned with
- ☐ a. avalanches.
- ☐ b. bad snowstorms.
- ☐ c. mountains.
- ☐ d. laughter.                                              _____

**Supporting Details**  **3**  Avalanches can be started by
- ☐ a. falling snow.
- ☐ b. the wind.
- ☐ c. loud sounds.
- ☐ d. friction between snowflakes.                          _____

**Conclusion**  **4**  We can conclude from this passage that avalanches
- ☐ a. are common everywhere.
- ☐ b. are not very common.
- ☐ c. have killed people.
- ☐ d. are a thing of the past.                              _____

**Clarifying Devices**  **5**  The writer compares an avalanche to
- ☐ a. a tornado.
- ☐ b. a falling house of cards.
- ☐ c. a snowstorm.
- ☐ d. a speeding train.                                     _____

**Vocabulary in Context**  **6**  In this passage <u>unstable</u> means
- ☐ a. frightening.
- ☐ b. fast.
- ☐ c. shaky.
- ☐ d. undesirable.                                          _____

**Add your scores for questions 1–6. Enter the total here**     **Total**
**and on the graph on page 216.**                               **Score**     _____

# 30 Abe's Favorite Story

If he hadn't turned to politics, Abe Lincoln might have done well as a comic. It has been said that he was always ready join in a laugh at his own <u>expense</u>. There is one particular story that he always told with great glee.

In his early days as a lawyer, Lincoln was on the "circuit." This meant going from town to town to hear and judge legal cases. During one of these many trips, he was sitting in a train when a strange man came up to him. The stranger looked at the tall, gawky lawyer quite sternly and explained that he had something he believed belonged to Lincoln. Lincoln was a bit confused. He had never seen the man before. He didn't see how a total stranger could have something of his. Lincoln asked him how this could be. The stranger pulled out a gleaming penknife and began to explain. Many years before, he had been given the pocketknife. He had been told to keep it until he was able to find a man uglier than himself.

Lincoln's eyes always sparkled when he reached this part of the story. He was never considered a handsome man. The stranger had decided that Lincoln was ugly enough to deserve the knife. The story always brought smiles to the faces of the audience that heard it. The tale itself was funny. But even more delightful was the fact that a man as great as Lincoln could still laugh at himself.

| Main Idea | 1 | | |
|-----------|---|---|---|
| | | Answer | Score |
| **Mark the *main idea*** | | M | 15 |
| **Mark the statement that is *too broad*** | | B | 5 |
| **Mark the statement that is *too narrow*** | | N | 5 |

a. Abe Lincoln used to tell a funny story that showed he could laugh at himself. ☐ _____

b. A good sense of humor can be a rare gift. ☐ _____

c. Lincoln's story makes fun of his ugliness. ☐ _____

**Score 15 points for each correct answer.**                    **Score**

**Subject Matter**    **2**    This passage is about
    ☐ a. Abe Lincoln's legal practice.
    ☐ b. a funny story that Abe Lincoln used to tell.
    ☐ c. the value of a penknife.
    ☐ d. traveling on trains.      _____

**Supporting**    **3**    As a tribute to his ugliness, Lincoln was given a
**Details**
    ☐ a. handshake.
    ☐ b. good laugh.
    ☐ c. penknife.
    ☐ d. train ticket.      _____

**Conclusion**    **4**    We can conclude that Lincoln's good sense of
    humor
    ☐ a. was frowned upon by most.
    ☐ b. made him a more popular person.
    ☐ c. was developed when we was a traveling
       lawyer.
    ☐ d. was the reason he was elected president.   _____

**Clarifying**    **5**    This passage
**Devices**
    ☐ a. gives many facts about Lincoln.
    ☐ b. gives a short history lesson.
    ☐ c. tells a story.
    ☐ d. is a fable.      _____

**Vocabulary**    **6**    In this passage the word <u>expense</u> means
**in Context**
    ☐ a. price.
    ☐ b. amount of money.
    ☐ c. charge.
    ☐ d. loss, or sacrifice.      _____

**Add your scores for questions 1–6. Enter the total here**    **Total**
**and on the graph on page 216.**    **Score**   _____

# 31 A Perfect Match

The first matches were made by a German experimenter. Like others of his time, he was trying to make gold. Instead, he came up with phosphorous. This chemical is so sensitive that it bursts into flame when exposed to the air. The first match was made in 1680. In those days, few people could afford even an ounce of phosphorous. It was so expensive that lighting a match was like burning money. The first matches were toys for the rich. They were not matches as we know them. They were small bottles containing pieces of paper dipped in phosphorous. When exposed to the air, they caught fire.

It was not until 1827, in England, that the type of match we are familiar with was made. It used phosphorous too, but in smaller amounts. It was lighted by friction. Everyone could afford these matches. They replaced flint and steel, which for ages had been the only tools for starting fires. But these matches proved to be a curse as well as a blessing. Phosphorous is a deadly poison. The people who made matches often died from a disease caused by the poison. Babies died from swallowing match heads. Some people used them to commit suicide.

At last, in 1911, William Fairburn devised a <u>nontoxic</u> type of phosphorous. He proved himself an unselfish man by giving the formula to all the matchmakers, rather than keeping it for his own profit.

| Main Idea | 1 | | Answer | Score |
|---|---|---|---|---|
| | **Mark the *main idea*** | | M | 15 |
| | **Mark the statement that is *too broad*** | | B | 5 |
| | **Mark the statement that is *too narrow*** | | N | 5 |

a. Matches went through many stages of development before the modern match was invented. ☐ _____

b. The phosphorous used in early matches was deadly poisonous. ☐ _____

c. Matches are made from chemicals. ☐ _____

**Score 15 points for each correct answer.**  **Score**

**Subject Matter**  2  This passage deals with
- ☐ a. the dangers of phosphorous.
- ☐ b. the invention of gold.
- ☐ c. the invention of matches.
- ☐ d. flint and steel.

_____

**Supporting Details**  3  Phosphorous was a good chemical to use for matches because it was very
- ☐ a. poisonous.
- ☐ b. expensive.
- ☐ c. flammable.
- ☐ d. fire resistant.

_____

**Conclusion**  4  Fairburn's decision to share his formula probably caused him to lose
- ☐ a. bets.
- ☐ b. friends.
- ☐ c. money.
- ☐ d. respect.

_____

**Clarifying Devices**  5  The author compares lighting one of the earliest matches to burning money in order to describe
- ☐ a. how unlikely it was that an inexpensive match could be made.
- ☐ b. how foolishly people spent their money.
- ☐ c. how expensive phosphorous was.
- ☐ d. how flammable phosphorous was.

_____

**Vocabulary in Context**  6  <u>Nontoxic</u> means
- ☐ a. unsafe.
- ☐ b. not poisonous.
- ☐ c. inexpensive.
- ☐ d. less flammable.

_____

**Add your scores for questions 1–6. Enter the total here and on the graph on page 216.**  **Total Score**  _____

# 32 The Great Invasion

In 1944 an event occurred that changed the course of history. It was the invasion of France by the Allied forces. This invasion was the beginning of the end of World War II.

By 1944 most of Western Europe was controlled by German armies. To free the people, the Allies carefully planned their attack. British, Canadian, and American troops would set out from England and sail across the English Channel. They would land on the mainland of Europe and take back the land the Germans had grabbed.

The Germans knew the invasion was coming. They did not know where or when. The Allies tried to fool their enemy, and they succeeded. The Germans thought the invasion would come through northern France or through Belgium. The Allies decided to land further south, along France's Normandy coast. The Germans had <u>fortified</u> this region with guns, land mines, and barbed wire fences. But their main troops weren't there.

Invasion Day was June 6, 1944. Some 175,000 men were carried one hundred miles across the water. With them came tanks, trucks, and fighter planes providing bombing support. The goal in the first few days was to gain control of five beaches. From there troops could move inland.

Some of the worst fighting was at Omaha Beach. Just beyond the beach, Allied soldiers had to climb steep cliffs to make sure German gunnery was not there. At Omaha, over two thousand men died or were injured.

But the invasion was successful. The Allies established a beachhead by the end of the first day. Within a year, the Germans would be defeated.

| Main Idea | 1 | | Answer | Score |
|---|---|---|---|---|
| | Mark the *main idea* | | M | 15 |
| | Mark the statement that is *too broad* | | B | 5 |
| | Mark the statement that is *too narrow* | | N | 5 |

a.  Sometimes an invasion can change history.  ☐  _____

b.  The Germans did not know where the invasion would take place.  ☐  _____

c.  The Allied invasion of France was an important turning point in World War II.  ☐  _____

**Subject Matter**    **2**    This passage mainly deals with
☐ a. how the invasion was planned and carried out.
☐ b. how the Germans got revenge.
☐ c. the problems at Omaha Beach.
☐ d. how one Allied soldier felt during the invasion.

_____

**Supporting Details**    **3**    The Germans expected that the attack would come through
☐ a. southern France.
☐ b. Belgium.
☐ c. England.
☐ d. Italy.

_____

**Conclusion**    **4**    It was necessary to gain control of the beaches
☐ a. so that more men and supplies could be landed.
☐ b. because many German troops were there.
☐ c. as a point of pride.
☐ d. because the troops that were landing didn't speak French.

_____

**Clarifying Devices**    **5**    When the passage says that the invaders had "established a beachhead," it means that they had
☐ a. set up a bathing area.
☐ b. gotten control of land along the beach.
☐ c. set up pit toilets.
☐ d. begun building a place to hold prisoners of war.

_____

**Vocabulary in Context**    **6**    <u>Fortified</u> means
☐ a. patrolled.
☐ b. entered.
☐ c. overrun.
☐ d. strengthened against attack.

_____

**Add your scores for questions 1–6. Enter the total here and on the graph on page 216.**    **Total Score**    _____

# 33 The Ship with Four Legs

There is just one four-legged animal that can walk two hundred miles without stopping once to rest. It would take a person two days and two nights to walk this far, and only one man has ever done it without stopping. What amazing animal has such endurance? The camel! The camel is well known for something else, too. It can cross an entire desert without a single drink of water. Its body is built in a special way to help it store water and food.

A person has just one stomach, but a camel has quite a few. Within each stomach are layers and layers of cells. These cells are like tiny water balloons, storing liquids until the camel needs them. When the camel drinks, the cells grow larger and larger. For a whole week, they can keep the animal's thirst away by sending water to all parts of its body.

Did you ever wonder why the camel has a hump? The hump is a storage place for fat. Because it has this storage area, the camel does not need to eat very often. When the animal needs energy, the layers of fat serve as fuel to keep it going on the long, hot days in the burning sun.

The camel has one other gift that makes it well suited to <u>arid</u> regions. This gift is its amazing nose. A camel can smell a water hole from miles away!

When a camel moves, it sways from side to side like a ship on a wavy ocean. Because of this swaying motion, the camel has been called the "Ship of the Desert."

| Main Idea | 1 | Answer | Score |
|---|---|---|---|
| | **Mark the *main idea*** | M | 15 |
| | **Mark the statement that is *too broad*** | B | 5 |
| | **Mark the statement that is *too narrow*** | N | 5 |
| | a. Desert animals have great endurance. | ☐ | ____ |
| | b. Camels can store liquids in their bodies for long periods. | ☐ | ____ |
| | c. The camel is built to survive in the desert. | ☐ | ____ |

**Subject Matter**   **2**    This passage is mainly about
- ☐ a. long-distance walking.
- ☐ b. mysterious ships.
- ☐ c. the camel.
- ☐ d. desert animals.

                                                     \_\_\_\_\_

**Supporting Details**   **3**    The camel's hump is a storage place for
- ☐ a. muscles.
- ☐ b. extra water.
- ☐ c. body sugars.
- ☐ d. fat.

                                                     \_\_\_\_\_

**Conclusion**   **4**    We can conclude from this passage that camels
- ☐ a. feel at home in the desert.
- ☐ b. like to carry heavy loads.
- ☐ c. look like ships from a distance.
- ☐ d. love to drink water.

                                                     \_\_\_\_\_

**Clarifying Devices**   **5**    The author compares cells with water balloons in order to
- ☐ a. make you think of summer.
- ☐ b. help you visualize the cells.
- ☐ c. show how rubber is elastic.
- ☐ d. show how many shapes cells can have.

                                                     \_\_\_\_\_

**Vocabulary in Context**   **6**    The word <u>arid</u> is closest in meaning to
- ☐ a. sunny.
- ☐ b. flat.
- ☐ c. dry.
- ☐ d. sandy.

                                                     \_\_\_\_\_

**Add your scores for questions 1–6. Enter the total here and on the graph on page 216.**          **Total Score**   \_\_\_\_\_

# 34  The Octopus Plant

Unless you have visited the southern United States, you probably have never heard of kudzu. Kudzu, as any farmer in the South will sadly tell you, is a super-powered weed. It is a strong climbing vine. Once it gets started, kudzu is almost impossible to stop. It climbs to the tops of the tallest trees. It can cover large buildings. Whole barns and farmhouses have been known to disappear from view. It has even been said to <u>engulf</u> small, slow-moving children, but that is probably an exaggeration. Still, wherever it grows, its thick, twisting vines are extremely hard to remove.

Kudzu was once thought to be a helpful plant. Originally found in Asia, it was brought to America to help fight erosion. It was planted where its tough roots, which grow up to five feet long, could help hold back the soil. But the plant soon spread to places where it wasn't wanted. Farmers now have to fight to keep it from eating up all the nutrients in the soil and killing other plants. In a way, it works as a sign of unemployment in the South; where there is no one to work the fields, kudzu soon takes over.

The northern United States faces no threat from kudzu. Harsh winters kill off its vines. The plant loves the warmth of the South. But the South surely doesn't love it. If someone could invent some use for kudzu and take it off southern farmers' lands, his or her fortune would be assured.

**Main Idea**    1

|  | Answer | Score |
|---|---|---|
| Mark the *main idea* | M | 15 |
| Mark the statement that is *too broad* | B | 5 |
| Mark the statement that is *too narrow* | N | 5 |

a.  Kudzu is a plant that was used to help fight soil erosion.    ☐ _____

b.  Kudzu is a fast-growing vine that has become a pest in the southern United States.    ☐ _____

c.  Southern farmers face many difficulties in raising crops.    ☐ _____

**Subject Matter**   **2**   This passage is mostly concerned with
- [ ] a. kudzu.
- [ ] b. farming.
- [ ] c. the South.
- [ ] d. soil erosion.

_____

**Supporting Details**   **3**   When fields are neglected in the South,
- [ ] a. erosion becomes a problem.
- [ ] b. farmers attack the kudzu.
- [ ] c. employment is bound to improve.
- [ ] d. kudzu soon grows over them.

_____

**Conclusion**   **4**   We can conclude from the passage that kudzu
- [ ] a. is more helpful than harmful.
- [ ] b. is more harmful than helpful.
- [ ] c. is spreading to the North.
- [ ] d. holds promise as a seasonal food.

_____

**Clarifying Devices**   **5**   The author makes a case against kudzu by
- [ ] a. citing opinions.
- [ ] b. predicting its future.
- [ ] c. describing its effects.
- [ ] d. criticizing its defenders.

_____

**Vocabulary in Context**   **6**   The word <u>engulf</u> means
- [ ] a. take root.
- [ ] b. confuse.
- [ ] c. completely cover.
- [ ] d. carry off.

_____

**Add your scores for questions 1–6. Enter the total here and on the graph on page 216.**          Total Score     _____

# 35 Monkey Do

Would you send a monkey to do your shopping for you? Sounds pretty strange, doesn't it? But monkeys can be trained to do some amazing things. Most people are aware that monkeys are one of nature's brainiest beasts. Scientists have been studying the <u>link</u> between monkeys and people for a long time. They have designed experiments that test the monkey's ability to perform simple human tasks.

In one test, a psychologist put two monkeys in cages beside each other. Each cage contained a vending machine. One cage had a machine that gave out water. The other had one that gave out food. Instead of real coins, each monkey was given a bag of black and white tokens. The black tokens worked only in the food machine. The white tokens worked in the machine with the water. In time, both animals were able to figure out which coin worked in which machine.

Then the test was made harder. The coins were taken away. The monkey with the water machine was not allowed to have any water for twenty-four hours. The food monkey was deprived of food. The next day, the coins were returned to the monkeys. This time, though, the monkey with the food machine was given water machine tokens, and the monkey with the water machine was given the tokens that worked the food machine. What did the two hungry monkeys do? These smart creatures simply reached through the bars of their cages and traded tokens.

| Main Idea | 1 | | |
|---|---|---|---|
| | | **Answer** | **Score** |
| **Mark the *main idea*** | | M | 15 |
| **Mark the statement that is *too broad*** | | B | 5 |
| **Mark the statement that is *too narrow*** | | N | 5 |

a. An experiment showed that monkeys are capable of reasoning intelligently. ☐ _____

b. Some animals are very smart. ☐ _____

c. Scientists have studied monkeys' intelligence for a long time. ☐ _____

**Subject Matter**    **2**    This passage deals with

☐ a. vending machines.

☐ b. an experiment with monkeys.

☐ c. monkeys that go shopping.

☐ d. why animals are kept in cages.     _____

**Supporting Details**    **3**    The black tokens worked for

☐ a. both machines.

☐ b. the food machine one day and the water machine the next.

☐ c. only the food machine.

☐ d. only the water machine.     _____

**Conclusion**    **4**    This experiment showed that monkeys can

☐ a. trick the scientists.

☐ b. survive without food and water for a day.

☐ c. solve problems.

☐ d. share with each other.     _____

**Clarifying Devices**    **5**    Most of the passage is devoted to

☐ a. an experiment.

☐ b. a strange story.

☐ c. a joke.

☐ d. advice.     _____

**Vocabulary in Context**    **6**    In this passage link means

☐ a. ring of a chain.

☐ b. problem.

☐ c. connection.

☐ d. differences.     _____

**Add your scores for questions 1–6. Enter the total here and on the graph on page 216.**    **Total Score**    _____

# 36 Courage and Skill

John Paul Jones was one of the founders of the United States Navy. During the American Revolution, the colonies were <u>desperate</u>. They needed men to lead their small ships against the British fleet. Jones was more than willing to fight.

John Paul Jones had once been a captain of a British merchant ship. In 1773, his crew mutinied. One member of the crew tried to gain control of the ship. Jones shot the man to death. The mutiny took place near the port of Tobago, an island in the Caribbean. Authorities there decided to have a trial. This meant certain death for John Paul Jones, since the whole crew would testify against him. One night during a thunderstorm, he escaped from the jail.

He fled to the United States and lived with a family named Jones. His real name was John Paul. He added the name of Jones to his, in honor of the family. He outwitted the British ships that were sent to hunt him down. And he did this with little more than his own courage and the skill of his crew.

When the American Revolution ended he went to serve in the Russian navy. There he fought the Turks and achieved one of the few major naval victories in the history of Russia. He died in Paris at the age of forty-five.

John Paul Jones is considered both an American and Russian hero, but the English considered him a fugitive.

| Main Idea | 1 | | Answer | Score |
|---|---|---|---|---|
| | Mark the *main idea* | | M | 15 |
| | Mark the statement that is *too broad* | | B | 5 |
| | Mark the statement that is *too narrow* | | N | 5 |

a. John Paul Jones once killed a member of his crew. ☐ _____

b. John Paul Jones was a successful naval fighter. ☐ _____

c. Many brave men fought in the American Revolution. ☐ _____

**Subject Matter**    **2**    Another good title for this passage would be
- ☐ a. John Paul Jones.
- ☐ b. A British Merchant Seaman.
- ☐ c. The Greatest Naval Fighter.
- ☐ d. Founder of the United States Navy.

       _____

**Supporting Details**    **3**    John Paul Jones won a major victory for the Russian navy against the
- ☐ a. French.
- ☐ b. British.
- ☐ c. Turks.
- ☐ d. Spanish.

       _____

**Conclusion**    **4**    You can conclude from this passage that Jones was
- ☐ a. thoughtful.
- ☐ b. fearful.
- ☐ c. kind.
- ☐ d. courageous.

       _____

**Clarifying Devices**    **5**    The passage is basically a
- ☐ a. biography of John Paul Jones.
- ☐ b. criticism of John Paul Jones.
- ☐ c. history of the United States Navy.
- ☐ d. comparison of the American and Russian navies.

       _____

**Vocabulary in Context**    **6**    <u>Desperate</u> means
- ☐ a. in great need.
- ☐ b. reckless.
- ☐ c. hopeless.
- ☐ d. skillful.

       _____

**Add your scores for questions 1–6. Enter the total here and on the graph on page 216.**    **Total Score**    _____

# 37 No Chance to Dream

The thought of not sleeping for twenty-four hours or more is not a pleasant one for most people. The amount of sleep that each person needs varies. In general, each of us needs about eight hours of sleep each day to keep our bodies healthy and happy. Some people, however, can get by with just a few hours of sleep at night.

It doesn't matter when or how much a person sleeps. But everyone needs some rest to stay alive. Few doctors would have thought that there might be an exception to this. Sleep is, after all, a very basic need. But a man named Al Herpin turned out to be a real exception, for supposedly he never slept!

Al Herpin was ninety years old when doctors came to his home in New Jersey. They hoped to <u>negate</u> the claims that he never slept. But they were surprised. Though they watched him every hour of the day, they never saw Herpin sleeping. He did not even own a bed. He never needed one.

The closest that Herpin came to resting was to sit in a rocking chair and read a half dozen newspapers. His doctors were baffled by this strange case of permanent insomnia. Herpin offered the only clue to his condition. He remembered some talk about his mother having been injured several days before he had been born. Herpin died at the age of ninety-four, never—it seems—having slept a wink.

| Main Idea | 1 | | | Answer | Score |
|---|---|---|---|---|---|
| | | Mark the *main idea* | | M | 15 |
| | | Mark the statement that is *too broad* | | B | 5 |
| | | Mark the statement that is *too narrow* | | N | 5 |
| | a. | Some people don't need to sleep. | | ☐ | ___ |
| | b. | Al Herpin managed to stay alive without ever sleeping. | | ☐ | ___ |
| | c. | Al Herpin was watched closely by doctors. | | ☐ | ___ |

**Subject Matter**   **2**   This passage centers on
- [ ] a. dream interpretation.
- [ ] b. patterns of sleep.
- [ ] c. Al Herpin's sleepless life.
- [ ] d. sleep and dreams.

_____

**Supporting Details**   **3**   One possible clue to Herpin's insomnia was
- [ ] a. his mother's injury before he was born.
- [ ] b. that he never got tired.
- [ ] c. his magnificent physical condition.
- [ ] d. that he got enough rest by rocking.

_____

**Conclusion**   **4**   Al Herpin's condition could be regarded as
- [ ] a. normal.
- [ ] b. curable.
- [ ] c. healthful.
- [ ] d. rare.

_____

**Clarifying Devices**   **5**   The expression "get by" in the last sentence of the first paragraph is
- [ ] a. a confusing expression
- [ ] b. a vulgar expression.
- [ ] c. an everyday expression.
- [ ] d. an improper expression.

_____

**Vocabulary in Context**   **6**   Negate is a synonym for
- [ ] a. support.
- [ ] b. disprove.
- [ ] c. hide.
- [ ] d. verify.

_____

**Add your scores for questions 1–6. Enter the total here and on the graph on page 216.**

**Total Score**   _____

# 38 The World's Oldest Sport

Most of us have heard of thoroughbred horses. But what does "thoroughbred" mean? It means a horse of a pure breed. In other words, a thoroughbred is a type of horse that has not been mixed with any other type of horse through breeding. Thoroughbred horses are the world's fastest racers. Long ago, three Arabian stallions were brought to England by King Charles II. They were the <u>ancestors</u> of all thoroughbreds known today. They were called Byerley Turk, Godolphin Barb, and Darley Arabian.

Horse racing is one of the oldest sports in the world. Rulers of all times have enjoyed breeding their own horses. In the Middle Ages, kings liked to watch their knights on horseback compete in tournaments. Because of this, horse racing is often called "the sport of kings."

There are many different kinds of horse races. Flat races are races that take place on grass or dirt tracks. They are called "flat" because the horse is not made to jump over any obstacles.

In another kind of race, called the steeplechase, a horse must jump at least eighteen fences. Steeplechasing gets its name from races once held in Ireland. In these events, the course was set between the church steeples of one village and the next. The most famous steeplechase in modern times is the Grand National, held in England.

| Main Idea | 1 | Answer | Score |
|---|---|---|---|
| | Mark the *main idea* | M | 15 |
| | Mark the statement that is *too broad* | B | 5 |
| | Mark the statement that is *too narrow* | N | 5 |

| | | | |
|---|---|---|---|
| a. | All thoroughbreds today are descended from three Arabian stallions. | ☐ | ____ |
| b. | People have used horses for many purposes. | ☐ | ____ |
| c. | Horse racing is one of the oldest sports in the world. | ☐ | ____ |

| | | |
|---|---|---|
| **Subject Matter** | **2** | This passage is mostly about |
| | | ☐ a. the Middle Ages. |
| | | ☐ b. Arabian stallions. |
| | | ☐ c. horseracing. |
| | | ☐ d. steeplechasing. |

| | | |
|---|---|---|
| **Supporting Details** | **3** | Steeplechasing gets its name from |
| | | ☐ a. races once held in Ireland. |
| | | ☐ b. horses that run toward steeples. |
| | | ☐ c. horses that run away from steeples. |
| | | ☐ d. horses that jump over high obstacles. |

| | | |
|---|---|---|
| **Conclusion** | **4** | From this passage, we can see |
| | | ☐ a. horse racing is a sport that only royalty enjoy. |
| | | ☐ b. horses love to race. |
| | | ☐ c. horseracing has been popular for a long time. |
| | | ☐ d. horseracing is only enjoyed in England. |

| | | |
|---|---|---|
| **Clarifying Devices** | **5** | "They could run like lightning" means the horses were |
| | | ☐ a. unpredictable. |
| | | ☐ b. electrifying. |
| | | ☐ c. dangerous. |
| | | ☐ d. fast. |

| | | |
|---|---|---|
| **Vocabulary in Context** | **6** | An <u>ancestor</u> is |
| | | ☐ a. a very close relative. |
| | | ☐ b. a thoroughbred horse. |
| | | ☐ c. a relative who lived long ago. |
| | | ☐ d. a horse that is very fast. |

**Add your scores for questions 1–6. Enter the total here and on the graph on page 216.**

**Total Score** _____

# 39 Glass on the Beach

If you have gone to the same seashore for several years, you may have noticed that the beach gets smaller every year. The wind and the waves carry the beach out to sea, bit by bit. Most shore towns try to fight the beach changes caused by ocean currents and the tides. Some dig sand out of the backwater bays and dump it on the beachfront. Others build wooden piers and jetties made to keep currents away from the beach.

A type of artificial sand that has been developed might be able to slow down beach erosion. Strangely, this new kind of sand is made of ground glass! You might think that walking barefoot on ground glass would be painful. But it's not. The reason is very simple. Sand and glass are made of the same kind of material, called silicate. When glass is ground very finely, you get a sandlike substance that is harder than real sand. The size of the pieces can be controlled. Larger pieces wouldn't be as easily affected by the wind and waves. So a beach covered with artificial sand would last longer than a beach with real sand.

A wonderful thing about artificial sand is that it can be made from waste glass. But making artificial sand costs three times as much as using <u>conventional</u> methods of beach protection. So it is not likely that sand made of glass will be used in the near future.

| Main Idea | 1 | | |
|---|---|---|---|
| | | **Answer** | **Score** |
| Mark the *main idea* | | M | 15 |
| Mark the statement that is *too broad* | | B | 5 |
| Mark the statement that is *too narrow* | | N | 5 |

a. Artificial sand can slow beach erosion. ☐ ____

b. Beaches are washed away by wind and waves. ☐ ____

c. Many things can be used to stop beaches from shrinking. ☐ ____

## Score 15 points for each correct answer.

**Subject Matter** **2** The subject of this passage is
- ☐ a. summer vacations.
- ☐ b. the seashore.
- ☐ c. artificial sand.
- ☐ d. sand and water.

_____

**Supporting Details** **3** Ground glass is
- ☐ a. hard to walk on.
- ☐ b. similar to sand but harder.
- ☐ c. difficult to make.
- ☐ d. found in nature.

_____

**Conclusion** **4** The passage suggests that artificial sand is
- ☐ a. not nice looking.
- ☐ b. the best way to slow down erosion.
- ☐ c. a foolish idea.
- ☐ d. too costly to ever be used.

_____

**Clarifying Devices** **5** In the first sentence, the author gets the reader's attention by
- ☐ a. referring to something the reader might be familiar with.
- ☐ b. telling a fact that is very humorous.
- ☐ c. saying something very surprising.
- ☐ d. asking a question.

_____

**Vocabulary in Context** **6** Conventional, as used in this passage, means
- ☐ a. old.
- ☐ b. standard.
- ☐ c. expensive.
- ☐ d. unusual.

_____

**Add your scores for questions 1–6. Enter the total here and on the graph on page 216.**

**Total Score** _____

# 40 The Monstrous Flower

Have you ever heard of a flower whose seeds are carried and spread by elephants? The rafflesia, a rare blossom, is very unusual. Found in the rain forests of Sumatra, the rafflesia is the world's largest flower, measuring three feet in diameter.

This giant flower is a parasite—it needs another plant to live on. It lacks the structures needed to survive alone. The rafflesia has no stem or leaves. It is all flower. It attaches itself to the roots of other plants and sucks their juices. The flower's favorite home is the root of the cissus vine, which grows above ground.

The rafflesia seems to burst right out of the forest floor. Its blossom weighs fifteen pounds! It has thick, spotted petals that give off a foul smell. The center, or nectary, is about the size of a household bucket. After a rain, it may hold up to twelve pints of water.

After the rafflesia dies, it becomes a pool of thick liquid in which seeds float. Elephants wandering through the forest step into the mushy pool, and the seeds glue themselves to their feet. As the animals stomp though the forest, their sticky feet pick up twigs and leaves. The elephants try to rid themselves of the sticky mess, in the same way people try to get bubble gum off their shoes. The elephants rub their feet against the roots of the cissus vine. In no time, seeds left on the vine grow into more monstrous flowers!

| Main Idea | 1 | | |
|---|---|---|---|
| | | Answer | Score |
| | Mark the *main idea* | M | 15 |
| | Mark the statement that is *too broad* | B | 5 |
| | Mark the statement that is *too narrow* | N | 5 |

a. The rafflesia is one of the world's most unusual flowers. ☐ _____

b. Some flowers grow in strange ways. ☐ _____

c. The rafflesia has no root structure of its own. ☐ _____

**Score 15 points for each correct answer.**

**Subject Matter**    **2**    This passage is about
- ☐ a. wandering elephants.
- ☐ b. the rafflesia.
- ☐ c. cissus vines.
- ☐ d. parasites.

_____

**Supporting Details**    **3**    Elephants help to
- ☐ a. provide food for the giant flower.
- ☐ b. water the rafflesia with their trunks.
- ☐ c. carry rafflesia seeds from one place to another.
- ☐ d. stomp out the awful smelling petals.

_____

**Conclusion**    **4**    From this passage, we can guess that the writer
- ☐ a. likes elephants.
- ☐ b. has a very large garden.
- ☐ c. admires the wonders of nature.
- ☐ d. likes to measure things.

_____

**Clarifying Devices**    **5**    To give us an idea of how large the rafflesia is, the author uses
- ☐ a. the size of an elephant for comparison.
- ☐ b. measurements.
- ☐ c. comparisons to other flowers.
- ☐ d. detailed descriptions of the flower's stem.

_____

**Vocabulary in Context**    **6**    As used in this passage <u>structures</u> means
- ☐ a. endurance.
- ☐ b. organization.
- ☐ c. necessary parts.
- ☐ d. energy.

_____

**Add your scores for questions 1–6. Enter the total here and on the graph on page 216.**

**Total Score** _____

# 41 Famous Horses of the Past

Did you think only kings and queens lived in marble houses? Well, Caligula, a Roman Emperor, kept his horse, Incitatus, in a marble stable! The horse's stall was made of ivory. The horse wore a golden collar inlaid with jewels. His purple blanket was a sign of royalty. It was rumored that Caligula had even made his horse consul! A consul was a ruler with much power.

Horses have helped to shape history. Long ago, winning or losing a battle often depended on how fast a horse could run. Horses were <u>crucial</u> in war. General Robert E. Lee never parted with his horse, Traveller. During the American Civil War, General Lee led the Confederate Army. Traveller braved many battles with Lee and was never hurt.

The most famous warhorse of all time was made of wood! It actually helped defeat an entire army. About 3,500 years ago, a fierce battle was going on between the Trojans and the ancient Greeks in a place called Asia Minor. The Greeks tried to think of a way to outsmart their enemies. Finally they built a huge wooden horse, taller than two houses, and left it outside the gates of the city of Troy. Since they didn't know where it came from, the Trojans thought the horse had magical powers. Carefully, they pulled it through the gates. That night, a surprising thing happened. The sides of the wooden horse opened and a band of Greek soldiers climbed out. They opened the gates of Troy and let in the Greek army. The Greeks soon captured the city of Troy.

**Main Idea**    1

| | Answer | Score |
|---|---|---|
| Mark the *main idea* | M | 15 |
| Mark the statement that is *too broad* | B | 5 |
| Mark the statement that is *too narrow* | N | 5 |

a. Horses are interesting animals. ☐ _____

b. Horses helped to shape history. ☐ _____

c. The most famous war horse was the Trojan horse. ☐ _____

**Subject Matter**   **2**   The subject matter of this passage is
- ☐ a. horses in history.
- ☐ b. horses of war.
- ☐ c. magical powers.
- ☐ d. Greek soldiers.    _____

**Supporting Details**   **3**   According to this passage, the Trojan horse
- ☐ a. had magical powers.
- ☐ b. was made of wood.
- ☐ c. led thousands of soldiers.
- ☐ d. was never wounded.    _____

**Conclusion**   **4**   The Trojans did not expect to find
- ☐ a. soldiers inside the horse.
- ☐ b. weapons inside the horse.
- ☐ c. such a wonderful gift.
- ☐ d. that the gods favored them.    _____

**Clarifying Devices**   **5**   The first sentence in the second paragraph tells what
- ☐ a. the author wants most to tell us in this passage.
- ☐ b. horses are usually raised for.
- ☐ c. can be done by an intelligent horse.
- ☐ d. must be done to train a war horse.    _____

**Vocabulary in Context**   **6**   If something is <u>crucial</u>, it is
- ☐ a. needed very much.
- ☐ b. difficult to understand.
- ☐ c. very fast.
- ☐ d. surprising.    _____

**Add your scores for questions 1–6. Enter the total here and on the graph on page 217.**    **Total Score**    _____

# 42 A Safe Place to Sleep

Need some sleep? Maybe you should try curling up in a cactus. This prickly plant can provide sound slumber—at least for a desert centipede. It has worked as a bedroom for this creature for years. The centipede is a long bug with one hundred legs. Although pretty scary to look at itself, the bug is afraid of the tarantula, a large dark spider with eight big hairy legs.

Each night before the centipede goes to sleep, it builds a special burglar alarm made of cactus. It surrounds itself with these sharp plants. The smart bug knows that the tarantula will never crawl over cactus. That would be like hugging a porcupine. So the centipede sleeps safely in its cactus corral. It can be sure that no enemy will get in.

Shut out by this prickly prison, the hungry tarantula lurks outside the centipede's bedroom for hours. First it circles the wall, then it peers over and circles again. Finally it decides that there is nothing it can do. It leaves the centipede to sleep and goes off to look for a creature that won't protect itself as well.

The next day the centipede wakes up from a good night's sleep, figuring the tarantula has surely given up by now. Still, the centipede is <u>cautious</u>. It takes a long and very careful look around. Only when it's sure that the coast is clear does the centipede begin to remove the wall of cactus that protected it in sleep.

## Main Idea 1

| | Answer | Score |
|---|---|---|
| Mark the *main idea* | M | 15 |
| Mark the statement that is *too broad* | B | 5 |
| Mark the statement that is *too narrow* | N | 5 |

a. The tarantula will not climb over cactus. ☐ _____

b. Some creatures have unique methods of protecting themselves. ☐ _____

c. Centipedes protect themselves when they sleep by surrounding themselves with a wall of cactus. ☐ _____

**Subject Matter**    **2**    This passage is about
- ☐ a. the danger of tarantulas.
- ☐ b. creatures of the desert.
- ☐ c. the centipede's unique form of protection.
- ☐ d. how to get to sleep. _____

**Supporting Details**    **3**    Despite their excellent forts, centipedes are still very
- ☐ a. small.
- ☐ b. slow.
- ☐ c. cautious.
- ☐ d. reckless. _____

**Conclusion**    **4**    We can conclude that tarantulas
- ☐ a. don't eat centipedes.
- ☐ b. are related to porcupines.
- ☐ c. try to attack centipedes every night.
- ☐ d. are smarter than centipedes. _____

**Clarifying Devices**    **5**    The writer compares climbing on cactus to
- ☐ a. walking over hot coals.
- ☐ b. going without eating for weeks.
- ☐ c. hugging a porcupine.
- ☐ d. sleeping on a pin cushion. _____

**Vocabulary in Context**    **6**    A centipede that is <u>cautious</u> is
- ☐ a. careful.
- ☐ b. afraid.
- ☐ c. fearsome.
- ☐ d. poisonous. _____

**Add your scores for questions 1–6. Enter the total here and on the graph on page 217.**    Total Score _____

# 43 The Ancient Cockroach

He was there to greet the dinosaurs when they arrived on earth. He is still with us 170 million years and billions of kitchens later. Rather than being honored, this <u>sage</u> is despised. Nobody likes a cockroach. Perhaps our hatred of this hearty insect is due to envy. No creature knows more about survival than the cockroach.

A cockroach can live in the middle of the desert or under a kitchen sink. Recently, roaches have been found living in TV sets—the parts that heat up provide warmth, and the wax in the set serves as food. Roaches can survive on almost anything from rose petals to laundry soap. They can even do without any food or water at all for up to a month.

Cockroaches like living with people because there's always food around. Even ships at sea are plagued by cockroaches. One sea captain offered a bottle of brandy to any sailor who could catch one thousand roaches on board the ship. The crew turned in 32,000 of the pests.

Many fancy poisons are used to kill roaches, but there is no hope of getting rid of them completely. So keep your food wrapped up as tightly as possible. But remember, the roach's existence is one of those creepy facts of life on earth.

| Main Idea | 1 | Answer | Score |
|---|---|---|---|
| | Mark the *main idea* | M | 15 |
| | Mark the statement that is *too broad* | B | 5 |
| | Mark the statement that is *too narrow* | N | 5 |

a. The cockroach is one of the world's great survivors. ☐ _____

b. The cockroach can eat almost anything. ☐ _____

c. It's amazing that some creatures have survived on earth for millions of years. ☐ _____

**Score 15 points for each correct answer.**　　　　Score

**Subject Matter**　**2**　Another good title for this passage would be
　　　　　☐ a. How Cockroaches Eat.
　　　　　☐ b. The Hearty Cockroach.
　　　　　☐ c. Pest Control.
　　　　　☐ d. Brandy Reward.　　　　_____

**Supporting**　**3**　Cockroaches that live in television sets eat
**Details**　　　　☐ a. laundry soap.
　　　　　☐ b. rose petals.
　　　　　☐ c. dust.
　　　　　☐ d. wax.　　　　_____

**Conclusion**　**4**　The first sentence of the passage suggests that
　　　　　☐ a. dinosaurs are older than cockroaches.
　　　　　☐ b. there was only one cockroach 170 million
　　　　　　　years ago.
　　　　　☐ c. cockroaches existed before dinosaurs.
　　　　　☐ d. cockroaches helped to kill off the dinosaurs.　_____

**Clarifying**　**5**　The author makes the point that cockroaches
**Devices**　　　can survive anywhere by presenting
　　　　　☐ a. detailed word pictures.
　　　　　☐ b. scientific studies.
　　　　　☐ c. several different facts.
　　　　　☐ d. horror stories.　　　　_____

**Vocabulary**　**6**　A <u>sage</u> is
**in Context**　　　☐ a. an herb.
　　　　　☐ b. someone old and wise.
　　　　　☐ c. a western bush.
　　　　　☐ d. a story.　　　　_____

**Add your scores for questions 1–6. Enter the total here**　Total
**and on the graph on page 217.**　　　Score　　_____

# 44 Without Hook and Line

The people of the Maori tribe of New Zealand take their tickling seriously. Their survival depends on their ability to tickle. Tickling might not sound like a very hard or useful activity. But for the Maori, tickling is an important way to get food. The Maori practice their own brand of tickling on fish.

There are many fish in the shallow coastal waters of New Zealand. They are a main staple in the diet of the Maori. To catch the fish, a fisherman must first walk slowly and quietly in the shallow water. But the fish are wary. They often hide near jagged rocks and coral reefs. They swim quickly from one hiding place to another. But sometimes the hiding fish will sleep. This is when they are most <u>vulnerable</u> to the Maori's entrancing tickle.

When he spots a sleeping fish, the keen-eyed fisherman is set to make his move. Very slowly and cautiously he bends down and starts to tickle his napping food. The sleeping fish responds to the tickle by wiggling from its hiding spot. With a quick movement, the Maori fisherman reaches for the stunned fish. He holds on as tightly as he can with both hands. Supper has been caught with a tickle. The Maori's fishing techniques may be unusual, but they have been successful for many centuries.

| Main Idea | 1 | | Answer | Score |
|---|---|---|---|---|
| | | **Mark the *main idea*** | M | 15 |
| | | **Mark the statement that is *too broad*** | B | 5 |
| | | **Mark the statement that is *too narrow*** | N | 5 |

a. The Maori have unusual methods of gathering food. ☐ _____

b. It is easy to tickle fish when they are sleeping. ☐ _____

c. The Maori catch fish by tickling them. ☐ _____

**Subject Matter**    **2**    Another good title for this passage would be

☐ a. The Maori Comedians.

☐ b. Fishing in New Zealand.

☐ c. The Tickling Tribe of New Zealand.

☐ d. Funny Fish.      _____

**Supporting Details**    **3**    The Maori catch their fish in the shallow waters of

☐ a. the lakes.

☐ b. a stream.

☐ c. the coast.

☐ d. a swamp.      _____

**Conclusion**    **4**    This passage might best be summed up by saying that

☐ a. the Maori are a curious tribe.

☐ b. the Maori are among the bravest people in the world.

☐ c. tickling fish is a valuable Maori skill.

☐ d. tickling fish is an exciting Maori sport.      _____

**Clarifying Devices**    **5**    The writer begins this passage by

☐ a. saying surprising things about tickling.

☐ b. telling a funny story.

☐ c. answering questions about tickling.

☐ d. describing the Maori tribe of New Zealand.      _____

**Vocabulary in Context**    **6**    <u>Vulnerable</u> means

☐ a. afraid of.

☐ b. surprised by.

☐ c. open to attack.

☐ d. ticklish.      _____

**Add your scores for questions 1–6. Enter the total here and on the graph on page 217.**      **Total Score**      _____

# 45 Watch Out for Quicksand!

While hiking in the swamplands of Florida, Fred Stahl watched Jack Pickett disappear before his eyes. Pickett had stepped onto what looked like an <u>innocent</u> patch of dry sand and then started to sink. Within fifteen minutes, Pickett had disappeared completely beneath the surface.

Pickett was a victim of quicksand. If you think quicksand is something found only in adventure novels or films, you're making a big mistake. And that mistake could cost you your life.

Geologist Gerard H. Matthes, who once escaped from quicksand himself, always gave this message to hikers: "Anyone who ever walks off the pavement should learn about quicksand." It can be found almost anywhere.

Here are some of Matthes's tips on how to prevent being helplessly sucked under by quicksand. First of all, if you step into quicksand that is firm enough, you may be able to run out. But you have to move fast. If, however, the sand pulls your legs in too quickly for you to escape this way, throw yourself flat on your back. That's right—you can actually float in quicksand. Don't make the common mistake of raising your arms. Resting on the surface, your arms can help you to float. Any movements you make should be slow and deliberate. Quick, jerky movements can cause you to be completely sucked in, just as Jack Pickett was. Try doing a slow breaststroke or slowly rolling yourself to firm ground. Above all, don't panic.

## Main Idea    1

|  | Answer | Score |
|---|---|---|
| Mark the *main idea* | M | 15 |
| Mark the statement that is *too broad* | B | 5 |
| Mark the statement that is *too narrow* | N | 5 |

a. Quicksand exists in many places, and you should know how to deal with it. ☐ _____

b. A hiker named Pickett was sucked into the quicksand in the Florida swamps. ☐ _____

c. There are many natural dangers that you should know about. ☐ _____

**Subject Matter**   **2**   This passage deals mainly with
- [ ] a. where quicksand is found.
- [ ] b. what causes quicksand.
- [ ] c. the facts about quicksand.
- [ ] d. dangers in the wilderness.

_____

**Supporting Details**   **3**   When stepping into quicksand, you should first try to run out because
- [ ] a. most quicksand is slower in trapping a victim than commonly believed.
- [ ] b. the sand may be firm enough to allow escape this way.
- [ ] c. it can't trap you if you keep moving.
- [ ] d. this is the only way you can escape.

_____

**Conclusion**   **4**   The passage implies that quicksand
- [ ] a. is found mostly in swamp areas.
- [ ] b. permits no escape.
- [ ] c. is only found in books and movies.
- [ ] d. is a serious danger.

_____

**Clarifying Devices**   **5**   In the first paragraph, the writer creates interest by using a
- [ ] a. dramatic example.
- [ ] b. broad statement.
- [ ] c. surprising comparison.
- [ ] d. humorous story.

_____

**Vocabulary in Context**   **6**   As used in the first paragraph, <u>innocent</u> means
- [ ] a. almost bare.
- [ ] b. very pure.
- [ ] c. not dangerous.
- [ ] d. highly dangerous.

_____

**Add your scores for questions 1–6. Enter the total here and on the graph on page 217.**     **Total Score**

_____

# 46 The Prince Tames a Horse

A horse named Bucephalus was offered for sale to Philip, King of Macedonia, in about 340 B.C. The king, his son Alexander, and many others went to see it. The horse appeared extremely fierce. No one could mount it. King Philip was displeased and said, "Take this wild creature away." But Alexander said, "What a horse they are losing because they lack the skill and spirit to manage him!" Philip turned and said, "Young man, you find fault with your elders as if you know more than they or could manage the horse better."

The prince quietly replied, "I know I can manage the horse better."

"If you should not be able to ride him, what will you give up?"

"I will pay the price of the horse."

The king agreed to the bet. Alexander grasped the horse's bridle and quickly turned him toward the sun so he would not see his shadow, which was what had disturbed him. While the <u>spirited</u> horse pranced, Alexander spoke softly and stroked him. Then he leaped lightly upon the horse's back. Without pulling the reins too hard or using a whip or spurs, he set Bucephalus to running. He pushed him on to a full gallop. Philip and his court looked on in great fear.

At the end of the field, Alexander suddenly wheeled the horse and raced back at tremendous speed. Loud shouts broke out from the group. Alexander's father, weeping with joy, kissed him and said, "My son, seek another kingdom that may be worthy of your abilities, for Macedonia is too small for you."

**Main Idea** 1

|  | Answer | Score |
|---|---|---|
| Mark the *main idea* | M | 15 |
| Mark the statement that is *too broad* | B | 5 |
| Mark the statement that is *too narrow* | N | 5 |

a. Alexander knew how to tame horses. ☐ ____

b. King Philip learned that Alexander had qualities that would make him great. ☐ ____

c. People with strength and courage can tame wild horses. ☐ ____

**Subject Matter**    **2**    This passage is about
- ☐ a. how Macedonians trained horses.
- ☐ b. a son being disrespectful to his father.
- ☐ c. Alexander's great strength of character.
- ☐ d. a boy named Alexander and his horse Bucephalus.

_____

**Supporting Details**    **3**    Alexander was able to manage the horse because he
- ☐ a. was the king's son.
- ☐ b. was stern and harsh with the animal.
- ☐ c. was afraid of losing the bet with his father.
- ☐ d. noticed something about the horse that others missed.

_____

**Conclusion**    **4**    The horse's name, Bucephalus, is Greek for "ox head." Based on the passage, you could infer that
- ☐ a. the Macedonians thought oxen more beautiful than horses.
- ☐ b. Bucephalus looked like an ox.
- ☐ c. perhaps the horse was "as stubborn as an ox."
- ☐ d. there was no particular reason for the name.

_____

**Clarifying Devices**    **5**    The author develops the main idea of this passage through the use of
- ☐ a. detailed descriptions.
- ☐ b. a list of facts.
- ☐ c. comparisons.
- ☐ d. a story that includes dialogue.

_____

**Vocabulary in Context**    **6**    The word <u>spirited</u> is used to mean
- ☐ a. ghostly.
- ☐ b. skittish.
- ☐ c. lively.
- ☐ d. religious.

_____

**Add your scores for questions 1–6. Enter the total here and on the graph on page 217.**      **Total Score**

_____

# 47 No Moisture Here!

They are the world's driest places. Sometimes rain doesn't fall there for years. These dry areas—deserts—cover about one-fifth of the earth's surface.

Perhaps you think of a desert as a place filled with sand. This is true of many deserts, but not all. Areas near the North and South poles are also considered deserts by some scientists. They define a desert as any area where the moisture that is lost, mostly by evaporation, is greater than the moisture that falls as rain or snow.

Many deserts are near the equator, where the air is dry and warm. Others are in regions blocked off from oceans by mountains. In these areas the moisture from the ocean winds evaporates as the winds pass over the mountains and cool off. But some deserts are found right next to oceans. Deserts usually form along coastlines if there is a cold current in the ocean water. The cold wind blowing across that current and onto the nearby land holds little moisture.

Most deserts get less than ten inches of rain a year. Because the land is so dry, the rain doesn't <u>penetrate</u> it; it just washes over the surface. Some deserts almost never get any rain. For instance, it rains in the Atacama Desert on the coast of Chile about once every hundred years!

Not many varieties of plants will grow in a desert. Some cactuses survive because they store water inside themselves after a rain. When it does rain, a desert landscape may flourish. Many plants will put forth bright and beautiful flowers.

| Main Idea | 1 | Answer | Score |
|---|---|---|---|
| | Mark the *main idea* | M | 15 |
| | Mark the statement that is *too broad* | B | 5 |
| | Mark the statement that is *too narrow* | N | 5 |

| | | |
|---|---|---|
| a. A desert is one of the earth's basic land forms. | ☐ | ____ |
| b. A desert is any location that loses more moisture than it gets. | ☐ | ____ |
| c. Sometimes desert plants will flower. | ☐ | ____ |

**Score 15 points for each correct answer.**     **Score**

**Subject Matter**     2     The purpose of this passage is to
☐ a. describe desert conditions.
☐ b. keep people from traveling across deserts.
☐ c. tell about the driest desert in the world.
☐ d. compare very dry and very wet climates.     _____

**Supporting Details**     3     If conditions are right, deserts may be found
☐ a. only near the equator.
☐ b. only near the North and South Poles.
☐ c. only along coastlines.
☐ d. throughout the world.     _____

**Conclusion**     4     It is clear that most deserts would be good places to
☐ a. build summer homes.
☐ b. plant food crops.
☐ c. look for water holes.
☐ d. carry extra water.     _____

**Clarifying Devices**     5     To make the point about deserts that never get rain, the author
☐ a. describes some flowering desert plants.
☐ b. uses the example of the Atacama Desert.
☐ c. discusses the effect of the equator.
☐ d. discusses the effect of winds over mountains.     _____

**Vocabulary in Context**     6     In this passage, <u>penetrate</u> means
☐ a. soak through.
☐ b. race across.
☐ c. dig holes in.
☐ d. fall on.     _____

**Add your scores for questions 1–6. Enter the total here and on the graph on page 217.**     **Total Score**     _____

# 48 Protected by Armor

Where can you find a cliff built entirely by animals? On the bottom of the ocean! Underwater reefs are huge walls made by tiny animals called corals. Because corals are very small, reefs take hundreds of years to build.

How do such small animals accomplish such a great task? The answer is simple. The reefs are <u>composed</u> of coral skeletons!

The coral animals are called "polyps." They have very soft bodies. Without some kind of "armor," they would be eaten by fish. To protect themselves, they build limestone shells around their bodies.

Coral polyps live in colonies. They connect themselves to each other and to the ocean floor. The corals build their limestone skeletons by taking a mineral called calcium out of the water and depositing it around themselves. The calcium deposits are very hard. As new coral polyps are born and attach themselves to the colony, the formation gets bigger. After a long while, a large reef has grown up.

The world's largest coral reef is longer than the state of New York. It is the Great Barrier Reef of Australia.

| Main Idea | 1 | | Answer | Score |
|---|---|---|---|---|
| | Mark the *main idea* | | M | 15 |
| | Mark the statement that is *too broad* | | B | 5 |
| | Mark the statement that is *too narrow* | | N | 5 |

a. Coral reefs are built from the skeletons of tiny ocean animals. ☐ _____

b. Sea creatures create many wonderful things under the surface of the ocean. ☐ _____

c. Coral polyps build their limestone shells from calcium found in the water. ☐ _____

**Subject Matter**    **2**    This passage is mainly about
☐ a. limestone.
☐ b. Australia.
☐ c. coral reefs.
☐ d. calcium.                                                     _____

**Supporting**    **3**    Coral polyps are
**Details**                 ☐ a. limestone deposits.
☐ b. tiny animals.
☐ c. minerals.
☐ d. long reefs.                                                  _____

**Conclusion**    **4**    Coral reefs take a long time to build because
☐ a. coral is rare.
☐ b. calcium is hard to eat.
☐ c. corals are tiny.
☐ d. the ocean is very deep.                                     _____

**Clarifying**    **5**    The writer helps you to visualize the length of
**Devices**                 the Great Barrier Reef by
☐ a. comparing it to the size of another place.
☐ b. describing how long it is.
☐ c. telling you its measurements.
☐ d. telling you how long it took to build.                      _____

**Vocabulary**    **6**    The word <u>composed</u> means
**in Context**              ☐ a. ruined.
☐ b. made up of.
☐ c. glued together.
☐ d. colored by.                                                 _____

**Add your scores for questions 1–6. Enter the total here**    **Total**
**and on the graph on page 217.**                               **Score**    _____

# 49 Knock! Knock!

Knock on wood. Woodpeckers do just that. This bird is an amazing creature: it pecks so hard and fast that its head looks like a blur. The woodpecker knocks on dead wood, looking for insects to eat. Its chisel-like beak chips away bark and decayed wood, and the violent tapping disturbs insects hidden in the tree's cavities. When the woodpecker reaches the insects' home, it spears its dinner with a barbed and sticky tongue.

The woodpecker pecks at a speed of 1,300 miles per hour. At this speed, the impact of the bird's beak hitting the wood is almost like that of a supersonic jet smashing into a mountain. Each peck takes just a thousandth of a second. The movement is quicker than the human eye can follow. Incredibly, the bird's cherry-sized brain is never injured from all this <u>furious</u> smashing.

There is a secret to the woodpecker's ability to withstand the great impact of its pecking. The secret lies in the woodpecker's neck muscles. They are so well coordinated that the head and beak move only in a straight line. This spreads the shock evenly though the bird's body and into the tree trunk. Pecking at even a slight angle would kill the woodpecker. Design experts are using this bird as a model. They hope to come up with a crash helmet that will better protect people's head from injuries.

| Main Idea | 1 | | Answer | Score |
|---|---|---|---|---|
| | Mark the *main idea* | | M | 15 |
| | Mark the statement that is *too broad* | | B | 5 |
| | Mark the statement that is *too narrow* | | N | 5 |

a. The woodpecker is specially built to survive the great shock of its hard, fast pecking. □ ____

b. Birds are specially adapted to their habitats and way of life. □ ____

c. The woodpecker pecks at a very great speed. □ ____

**Score 15 points for each correct answer.**  Score

**Subject Matter**  2  The subject of this passage is
☐ a. knocking on wood.
☐ b. woodpeckers.
☐ c. whiplash.
☐ d. designing crash helmets.  _____

**Supporting Details**  3  The woodpecker doesn't get injured while pecking because it
☐ a. has a small brain.
☐ b. has specially adapted neck muscles.
☐ c. knocks only on dead wood.
☐ d. pecks faster than the eye can follow.  _____

**Conclusion**  4  The writer concludes that
☐ a. woodpeckers are well liked.
☐ b. people are annoyed by the tapping noise of woodpeckers.
☐ c. scientists can benefit from the study of woodpeckers.
☐ d. woodpeckers are important to the ecology of the forest.  _____

**Clarifying Devices**  5  The writer tries to demonstrate the great impact of a peck with
☐ a. a comparison.
☐ b. a story.
☐ c. an example.
☐ d. a definition.  _____

**Vocabulary in Context**  6  <u>Furious</u> pecking is
☐ a. angry.
☐ b. needless.
☐ c. unbearable.
☐ d. violent.  _____

**Add your scores for questions 1–6. Enter the total here and on the graph on page 217.**  Total Score  _____

# 50 Never Say Die

On October 17, 1829, Sam Patch did what he had said he would do. He perched on a platform built beside Niagara Falls and jumped into the water a hundred feet below. A big crowd had gathered to watch Sam's well-advertised leap. The spectators held their breath as the daredevil hit the swirling water. At last his head burst out of the foam, thirty feet clear of the falls, and the crowd let out a mighty roar. Men waved their hats and yelled out the expression that had become Sam's trademark: "There's no mistake in Sam Patch!"

Sam began his career as a leaper in 1827, when he jumped eighty feet into the Passaic River from a bridge that was still under construction. Delighted with the notoriety he received, Sam traveled from town to town, jumping from masts, cliffs, and bridges. Then he made his great conquest of Niagara Falls.

Sam was spurred on by the widespread public excitement over his successful leap from the falls. He turned to the higher Genesee Falls for his next feat. On November 13, a scaffold was constructed 125 feet above the base of the falls. A huge crowd gathered on both riverbanks. At 2:00 P.M., Sam climbed the shaky scaffold, made a brief speech, and jumped. Once again there was a hushed silence as his body smacked the water. But this time Sam didn't resurface.

Sam's body was pulled from the mouth of the river the following spring. Even so, for years afterward, a legend persisted that the great Sam Patch was still alive.

| Main Idea | 1 | | |
|---|---|---|---|
| | | **Answer** | **Score** |
| **Mark the *main idea*** | | M | 15 |
| **Mark the statement that is *too broad*** | | B | 5 |
| **Mark the statement that is *too narrow*** | | N | 5 |

a. Sam Patch died jumping the Genesee Falls. ☐ _____

b. Jumping from great heights is dangerous. ☐ _____

c. Sam Patch made a career of leaping from great heights. ☐ _____

**Subject Matter**    **2**    What is the general idea of the passage?
- ☐ a. Genesee Falls is a dangerous place.
- ☐ b. Sam Patch jumped at Niagara Falls.
- ☐ c. There's no mistake in Sam Patch.
- ☐ d. Sam Patch was a popular leaper.    _____

**Supporting Details**    **3**    Sam jumped into the Passaic River from a
- ☐ a. cliff.
- ☐ b. scaffold.
- ☐ c. bridge.
- ☐ d. mast.    _____

**Conclusion**    **4**    The passage implies that
- ☐ a. Sam Patch is still alive.
- ☐ b. Sam Patch was a foolish man.
- ☐ c. jumping from high bridges was not very dangerous.
- ☐ d. Sam Patch loved to get a lot of attention.    _____

**Clarifying Devices**    **5**    "Swirling" water is
- ☐ a. very rough.
- ☐ b. cold.
- ☐ c. boiling.
- ☐ d. deep.    _____

**Vocabulary in Context**    **6**    The best definition for the word <u>notoriety</u> is
- ☐ a. congratulations.
- ☐ b. payment.
- ☐ c. fame.
- ☐ d. pleasure.    _____

**Add your scores for questions 1–6. Enter the total here and on the graph on page 217.**    **Total Score**    _____

# 51 Leaf-Cutters

A clean dirt path several inches wide is a sign that you are near a leaf-cutter ant colony. In one direction the path branches into trails that end at a tree trunk or peter out in the grass. In the other direction it leads to the colony's nest—a wide area marked by holes and large rubbish heaps.

The holes are entrances to the underground nest. The rubbish heaps are piles of old, dry plant matter that was cleared out of the nest when it was no longer useful. Leaf-cutters are farmers, and they use leaves and grass to grow their food—fungi. Fungi are plants that grow on other plants or on decaying matter. Toadstools and molds are types of fungi. At night the ants go out to <u>forage</u> for more material to grow food. Each ant carries a piece of leaf at least twice as large as its own body.

Leaf-cutters come in all sizes, and, oddly enough, it is the largest ones who do the least work. They are soldiers, whose main job is to protect the nest. They have enormous jaws. Because of this, the native Indians of South America, where these ants are found, put them to an odd use. Instead of using stitches to close a wound, the Indians hold large leaf-cutter ants up to the edges of a cut and let them bite it together. Then they pinch off the bodies, leaving the jaws behind to hold the wound firmly closed.

| Main Idea | 1 | | | Answer | Score |
|---|---|---|---|---|---|
| | | Mark the *main idea* | | M | 15 |
| | | Mark the statement that is *too broad* | | B | 5 |
| | | Mark the statement that is *too narrow* | | N | 5 |

| | | Answer | Score |
|---|---|---|---|
| a. | The leaf-cutters are farmers that grow their food in dead plant material. | ☐ | ____ |
| b. | Leaf-cutter ants work hard to survive. | ☐ | ____ |
| c. | Leaf-cutters carry grass and leaves to their nests. | ☐ | ____ |

**Subject Matter**    **2**    This passage is about
- ☐ a. fungi.
- ☐ b. leaf-cutter ants.
- ☐ c. South American Indians.
- ☐ d. farming.      _____

**Supporting Details**    **3**    Leaf-cutter ants eat
- ☐ a bark from tree trunks.
- ☐ b. fungi.
- ☐ c. leaves and grass.
- ☐ d. decaying matter.      _____

**Conclusion**    **4**    This passage implies that
- ☐ a. leaf-cutter ants work harder than other ants.
- ☐ b. leaf-cutter ants are small.
- ☐ c. the largest ants do not help grow food for the colony.
- ☐ d. anyone can find a leaf-cutter colony.      _____

**Clarifying Devices**    **5**    The phrase "oddly enough" indicates
- ☐ a. from a human point of view it's strange that the strongest ants do the least work.
- ☐ b. small ants are lazy when compared with the larger ones.
- ☐ c. the ants vary in size tremendously, depending on their jobs.
- ☐ d. that it's odd that leaf cutters come in all sizes.      _____

**Vocabulary in Context**    **6**    To <u>forage</u> means to
- ☐ a. plant.
- ☐ b. work.
- ☐ c. search.
- ☐ d. beg.      _____

**Add your scores for questions 1–6. Enter the total here and on the graph on page 217.**     **Total Score**    _____

# 52 A Hard and Beautiful Mineral

What is the world's hardest natural substance? If you guessed something like iron or marble, you would be wrong. The world's hardest substance is actually the diamond.

Diamonds are formed deep in the earth and hardened by the intense heat and pressure found there. That pressure pushes the diamond material up near the surface into outlets called pipes. There the material cools off, and from there diamonds can be mined.

To bring out a diamond's brilliance, the stone must be cut and polished. The most valuable diamonds are clear—there are no dull spots in them. They are also colorless. (A few diamonds are pink or some other color, but these are rare and very expensive.) Valuable diamonds are fairly large, at the very least one <u>carat</u> in weight. And they are also well cut. This means they have even-sided faces, or facets, that reflect light clearly and evenly.

If diamonds are so hard, what is used to cut them? You guessed it: other diamonds. Many factories also use diamonds to cut other hard substances. Diamonds are used in polishing as well. Polishing material made of diamond particles can be used like sandpaper. It can make steel surfaces so smooth that they reflect like fine mirrors.

The world has always valued diamonds. People have fought over them, and curses have been placed on them. They are a symbol of power as well as love.

| Main Idea | 1 | Answer | Score |
|---|---|---|---|
| | Mark the *main idea* | M | 15 |
| | Mark the statement that is *too broad* | B | 5 |
| | Mark the statement that is *too narrow* | N | 5 |

a. Diamonds are the world's hardest natural substance. ☐ _____

b. Diamonds are valued for their hardness, beauty, and use in industry. ☐ _____

c. A clear diamond is a valuable diamond. ☐ _____

**Subject Matter** 2 Another good title for this passage would be
☐ a. How to Mine Diamonds.
☐ b. Diamonds: Beautiful and Useful.
☐ c. A Diamond in the Rough.
☐ d. Diamonds and Other Precious Stones.

_____

**Supporting Details** 3 For diamonds to be valuable, they must be
☐ a. pink.
☐ b. not more than one carat.
☐ c. pear-shaped.
☐ d. well cut.

_____

**Conclusion** 4 The diamonds used in industry are
☐ a. harder than those used as gemstones.
☐ b. of lower quality than those used as gemstones.
☐ c. extremely large.
☐ d. later used as gemstones.

_____

**Clarifying Devices** 5 Surfaces polished by diamonds are compared to
☐ a. stones.
☐ b. fine mirrors.
☐ c. carats.
☐ d. pipes.

_____

**Vocabulary in Context** 6 The word <u>carat</u> refers to a type of
☐ a. food.
☐ b. diamond.
☐ c. brightness.
☐ d. weight.

_____

**Add your scores for questions 1–6. Enter the total here and on the graph on page 217.**  **Total Score**

_____

# 53 No Runs, No Hits, and Too Many Errors

Some days it just doesn't pay to go to the ballpark. One day in 1966, Los Angeles Dodger outfielder Willie Davis was thinking of places he'd rather have been. At the time, anywhere must have seemed more inviting. The game he would like to have skipped was no ordinary test. It was the World Series.

The year 1966 had been a good one for the Dodgers. They had clinched the National League Pennant with ease, and all that was left was the World Series against the Baltimore Orioles. As far as most fans and sportswriters were concerned, the "Fall Classic" would be no contest. The Dodgers had powerful hitting and a pitcher who threw the ball so fast that some people insisted it could cause a sonic boom. But something unexpected happened. The Orioles' pitching sparkled, and their hitters were slugging the ball over the outfield fences. All the Dodger fans could talk about was the "cold Dodger bats"—that is, when they weren't talking about Willie Davis and "that inning." In this particular game Davis set a major league <u>record</u>, one that no ball player would be proud of. In one short inning he made three errors. He let an easy hit skid by him. Several pitches later, he lost a fly ball in the glare of the sun. And if that weren't bad enough, he picked up the ball he had missed and threw it over the infielder's head. Davis felt bad, but he wasn't alone. The Dodgers lost the best-out-of-seven series without winning a single game.

| Main Idea | 1 | | Answer | Score |
|---|---|---|---|---|
| | Mark the *main idea* | | M | 15 |
| | Mark the statement that is *too broad* | | B | 5 |
| | Mark the statement that is *too narrow* | | N | 5 |
| | a. Willie Davis had a bad day. | | ☐ | _____ |
| | b. Davis set a record by making three errors in one World Series inning. | | ☐ | _____ |
| | c. Willie Davis played for the Los Angeles Dodgers in the World Series. | | ☐ | _____ |

**Score 15 points for each correct answer.**     Score

Subject Matter     **2**     This passage deals with
☐ a. baseball fielding lessons.
☐ b. a bad dream.
☐ c. an unfortunate major league record.
☐ d. the city of Los Angeles.

_____

Supporting     **3**     Davis couldn't catch one of the fly balls because of
Details
☐ a. a back problem.
☐ b. the glare of the sun.
☐ c. a hole in his mitt.
☐ d. another fielder who got in the way.

_____

Conclusion     **4**     From reading this passage, we can conclude that because of his mistakes that day, Willie Davis was
☐ a. thrown off the team.
☐ b. arrested.
☐ c. embarrassed.
☐ d. ignored by his teammates.

_____

Clarifying     **5**     The term "cold Dodger bats" refers to
Devices
☐ a. poor hitting.
☐ b. winter weather that canceled a game.
☐ c. a new technique of cooling the baseball bats.
☐ d. flying creatures which plague Dodger Stadium.

_____

Vocabulary     **6**     In this passage, <u>record</u> means
in Context
☐ a. to put on tape.
☐ b. a disc with music on it.
☐ c. a performance surpassing all others.
☐ d. a written document.

_____

**Add your scores for questions 1–6. Enter the total here and on the graph on page 217.**     Total
Score

_____

# 54 The Code Talkers

Many people enjoy secret codes. The harder the code, the more some people will try to figure it out. In wartime, codes are especially important. They help armies send news about battles and the size of enemy forces. Neither side wants its code broken by the other.

One very important code was never broken. It was used during World War II by the Americans. It was a spoken code, never written down. And it was developed and used by Navajo Indians. They were called the "Navajo Code Talkers."

The Navajos created the code in their own language. Navajo is hard to learn, and only a few people know it. So it was pretty certain that the enemy would not be able to understand the Code Talkers. In addition, the Talkers used code words. They called a submarine an "iron fish" and a grenade a "potato." If they wanted to spell something, they used code words for letters of the alphabet. For instance, the letter *a* was "ant" or "apple" or "axe."

The Code Talkers worked mostly in the islands in the Pacific. One or two would be assigned to a <u>battalion</u> of soldiers. They would send messages by field telephone to the Code Talker in the next battalion. And he would relay the information to his commander.

The Code Talkers played an important part in several battles. They helped troops coordinate their movements and attacks. After the war, the U.S. government honored them for what they had accomplished. Theirs was the most successful wartime code ever used.

| Main Idea | 1 | | Answer | Score |
|---|---|---|---|---|
| | **Mark the *main idea*** | | M | 15 |
| | **Mark the statement that is *too broad*** | | B | 5 |
| | **Mark the statement that is *too narrow*** | | N | 5 |

| | | Answer | Score |
|---|---|---|---|
| a. | Many Navajo code terms were descriptions of objects. | ☐ | _____ |
| b. | The Navajo Code Talkers had an important job in World War II. | ☐ | _____ |
| c. | A good code is one that is hard or impossible to break. | ☐ | _____ |

**Score 15 points for each correct answer.**

**Subject Matter**   **2**   The subject of this passage is
    ☐ a. how the Navajo code worked during World War II.
    ☐ b. the kinds of words used as code words.
    ☐ c. the war in the Pacific.
    ☐ d. the bravery of the Code Talkers.    _____

**Supporting Details**   **3**   Instead of saying the letter *a,* the Code Talkers might say
    ☐ a. admiral.
    ☐ b. aircraft.
    ☐ c. axe.
    ☐ d. anteater.    _____

**Conclusion**   **4**   To do their jobs well, Code Talkers had to be fluent in Navajo and
    ☐ a. English.
    ☐ b. Japanese.
    ☐ c. German.
    ☐ d. sign language.    _____

**Clarifying Devices**   **5**   The writer explains how the code worked by
    ☐ a. telling a story.
    ☐ b. giving examples of code words.
    ☐ c. having two characters speak it.
    ☐ d. describing the Navajo language.    _____

**Vocabulary in Context**   **6**   A batallion is a
    ☐ a. code.
    ☐ b. group.
    ☐ c. hiding place.
    ☐ d. dining hall.    _____

**Add your scores for questions 1–6. Enter the total here and on the graph on page 217.**    Total Score    _____

# 55 Feeling the Forecast

To find out what the weather is going to be, most people go straight to the radio, television, or newspaper to get an expert weather forecast. But if you know what to look for, you can use your own senses to make weather predictions.

There are many signs that can help you. For example, in fair weather the air pressure is generally high, the air is still and often full of dust, and faraway objects may look hazy. But when a storm is brewing, the pressure drops and you are often able to see things more clearly. Sailors took note of this long ago and came up with a saying: "The farther the sight, the nearer the rain."

Your sense of smell can also help you detect weather changes. Just before it rains, odors become stronger. This is because odors are <u>repressed</u> in a fair, high-pressure center. When a bad weather low moves in, air pressure lessens and odors are released.

You can also hear an approaching storm. Sounds bounce off heavy storm clouds and return to earth with increased force. An old saying describes it this way: "Sound traveling far and wide, a stormy day will betide."

And don't scoff if your grandmother says she can feel a storm coming. It is commonly known that many people feel pains in their bones or in corns and bunions when the humidity rises, the pressure drops, and bad weather is on the way.

| Main Idea | 1 | Answer | Score |
|---|---|---|---|
| Mark the *main idea* | | M | 15 |
| Mark the statement that is *too broad* | | B | 5 |
| Mark the statement that is *too narrow* | | N | 5 |

|  |  |  |
|---|---|---|
| a. You can use your senses to detect weather changes. | ☐ | ____ |
| b. Seeing and hearing approaching storms is possible. | ☐ | ____ |
| c. With a little training, we can use our senses more effectively. | ☐ | ____ |

**Score 15 points for each correct answer.**           **Score**

**Subject Matter**   **2**   The topic of this passage is
    ☐ a. expert weather forecasters.
    ☐ b. seeing approaching storms.
    ☐ c. old sayings about weather.
    ☐ d. using the senses to detect weather changes.   _____

**Supporting Details**   **3**   According to the passage, as a storm approaches, faraway objects look
    ☐ a. hazy because of dust in the air.
    ☐ b. clearer because air pressure is high.
    ☐ c. clearer because air pressure is dropping.
    ☐ d. distorted because of cloud storms.   _____

**Conclusion**   **4**   In the last paragraph, the writer implies that
    ☐ a. the idea of feeling a coming storm is foolish.
    ☐ b. older people know a lot about weather.
    ☐ c. it is possible, but unlikely, that people feel aches when a storm is coming.
    ☐ d. it is definitely true that some people can feel coming weather changes.   _____

**Clarifying Devices**   **5**   The writer quotes the old saying "The farther the sight, the nearer the rain" in order to
    ☐ a. show how foolish and untrue such sayings were.
    ☐ b. show that this observation, made long ago, is true.
    ☐ c. convince the reader that expert predictions are not reliable.
    ☐ d. give the reader a visual image.   _____

**Vocabulary in Context**   **6**   As used in this passage, repressed is closest in meaning to
    ☐ a. spread out.
    ☐ b. composed.
    ☐ c. trapped.
    ☐ d. hidden.   _____

**Add your scores for questions 1–6. Enter the total here and on the graph on page 217.**   **Total Score**   _____

**111**

# 56 The African Elephant

The elephant is the largest of all land animals. It can reach a height of eleven feet and weigh nearly six tons. The African elephant can also boast the biggest ears in the world. They can grow as large as three-and-a-half feet across. You might think that a gigantic animal like the elephant wouldn't have much to worry about, but it has its problems too. And its huge ears can help it to deal with many problems ranging from pesky insects to great danger.

The ears are very effective fans that can be used to swat flies. The elephants' huge ears also help them hear everything that's happening nearby. A mother elephant might hear the approach of a dangerous lion that would kill her calves.

The elephants' great size can sometimes present a heat problem. The larger an object, the harder it is for it to lose heat. Elephants live on the hot plains of Africa, where keeping cool is not an easy task. Elephants' huge ears help them cool their bodies so they can survive in the heat. The large surfaces of the ears have many blood vessels that are very close to the surface of the skin. Blood that is closer to the surface cools more easily.

The most impressive use of the ears, though, is seen in an elephant's threat display. When trying to threaten another animal, the elephant bellows and charges with both ears spread wide. This makes the huge beast look almost twice as large as it really is. Few enemies would dare to stand up to anything that <u>colossal</u>.

| Main Idea | 1 | | | |
|---|---|---|---|---|
| | | | Answer | Score |
| | Mark the *main idea* | | M | 15 |
| | Mark the statement that is *too broad* | | B | 5 |
| | Mark the statement that is *too narrow* | | N | 5 |
| | a. Large ears help animals survive. | | ☐ | _____ |
| | b. African elephants lose heat through their ears. | | ☐ | _____ |
| | c. The huge ears of African elephants help them in many ways. | | ☐ | _____ |

**Subject Matter**   **2**   Another good title for this passage would be
- ☐ a. Survival on the African Plains.
- ☐ b. They're All Ears.
- ☐ c. Keeping Cool in Africa.
- ☐ d. The Elephant's Threat Display.

        \_\_\_\_\_

**Supporting Details**   **3**   The African elephant's large ears help it to
- ☐ a. hide.
- ☐ b. cool off.
- ☐ c. find food.
- ☐ d. control its young.

        \_\_\_\_\_

**Conclusion**   **4**   We can conclude that if elephants did not have big ears they would probably
- ☐ a. see better.
- ☐ b. be smaller.
- ☐ c. not be able to survive.
- ☐ d. not live in Africa.

        \_\_\_\_\_

**Clarifying Devices**   **5**   The author calls the elephant's threat display "impressive." This means that it is
- ☐ a. interesting.
- ☐ b. admirable.
- ☐ c. amusing.
- ☐ d. normal.

        \_\_\_\_\_

**Vocabulary in Context**   **6**   <u>Colossal</u> indicates that the elephant appears
- ☐ a. extremely angry.
- ☐ b. incredibly large.
- ☐ c. to be moving very fast.
- ☐ d. amazingly strong.

        \_\_\_\_\_

**Add your scores for questions 1–6. Enter the total here and on the graph on page 217.**   **Total Score**   \_\_\_\_\_

# 57 Jaws

Of all the fish in the ocean, sharks are the greediest eaters and killers. They suffer from <u>continual</u> hunger. Almost as soon as they have eaten, they are on the prowl for more food. Sharks have been described as eating machines, and indeed they are perfectly designed for that activity. They are powerful swimmers, with smooth, well-muscled, streamlined bodies.

But the most remarkable part of a shark is its mouth—a wide gash lined with rows of jagged teeth. When a shark attacks, it opens its mouth wide until its teeth can stab straight into the body of its victim. The teeth slice like razors as the shark twists and rolls its body to tear off a chunk of food. New teeth are constantly being formed and moving forward to take the place of those lost during the shark's violent feeding activities. Even very old sharks have razor-sharp teeth.

The largest and most fearsome of the species is the great white shark. Its average length is between fourteen and sixteen feet. A few great whites may reach well over thirty feet in length. The longest ever recorded was a thirty-seven-footer, a truly monstrous fish. The great white lives in the tropical seas and sometimes along the southern coast of the United States.

| Main Idea | 1 | Answer | Score |
|---|---|---|---|
| | Mark the *main idea* | M | 15 |
| | Mark the statement that is *too broad* | B | 5 |
| | Mark the statement that is *too narrow* | N | 5 |
| a. | Sharks are large ocean fish. | ☐ | _____ |
| b. | Sharks are greedy eaters. | ☐ | _____ |
| c. | Sharks are powerful fish well designed to hunt other fish for food. | ☐ | _____ |

**Subject Matter**  **2**  This passage is mostly about
- [ ] a. great white sharks.
- [ ] b. how sharks are designed for their eating needs.
- [ ] c. the way in which sharks grow new teeth.
- [ ] d. why so many people hate and fear sharks.        _____

**Supporting Details**  **3**  Sharks tear off food by
- [ ] a. squeezing it.
- [ ] b. slicing it.
- [ ] c. killing it.
- [ ] d. rolling their bodies.        _____

**Conclusion**  **4**  We can infer from this passage that
- [ ] a. even old sharks have no trouble eating.
- [ ] b. old sharks starve to death because of weak teeth.
- [ ] c. sharks fear people and will not go near them.
- [ ] d. sharks die young because they wear themselves out.        _____

**Clarifying Devices**  **5**  "Jagged" teeth are
- [ ] a. dull.
- [ ] b. broken.
- [ ] c. sharp and uneven.
- [ ] d. large.        _____

**Vocabulary in Context**  **6**  <u>Continual</u> means
- [ ] a. painful.
- [ ] b. fierce.
- [ ] c. constant.
- [ ] d. enormous.        _____

**Add your scores for questions 1–6. Enter the total here and on the graph on page 217.**        **Total Score**        _____

# 58 Are You Superstitious?

Many superstitious people are afraid of black cats. They believe that black cats have a strange power. If a black cat crosses their path, they think they will have bad luck.

Black cats haven't always had such a bad reputation. Long ago, the Egyptians thought that black cats were holy animals. They even worshipped them. Pasht was an Egyptian goddess who had a woman's body and a cat's head. Because the Egyptians had so much respect for black cats, they often buried the <u>sacred</u> creatures with great ceremony. Mummies of cats have often been found in ancient cemetery ruins. To keep the cats company after they died, mice were sometimes buried beside them.

Feelings about black cats have always been strong. People have thought they were either very good or very bad. The people of Europe in the Middle Ages believed black cats were the evil friends of witches and the devil. Witches were said to have the power to change themselves into black cats. People believed that you could not tell whether a black cat was just a cat or whether it was a witch disguising herself as she plotted some evil scheme. The brain of a black cat was thought to be a main ingredient in a witch's brew.

Unlike their ancestors of the Middle Ages, the English today consider black cats to be good luck charms. Fishermen's wives often keep a black cat around so that their husbands will be protected when they are out at sea.

| Main Idea | 1 | | |
|---|---|---|---|
| | | **Answer** | **Score** |
| | Mark the *main idea* | M | 15 |
| | Mark the statement that is *too broad* | B | 5 |
| | Mark the statement that is *too narrow* | N | 5 |

a. People think that cats are special animals. ☐ _____

b. Black cats have always been thought to have special powers. ☐ _____

c. Superstitious people believe that black cats bring bad luck. ☐ _____

**Subject Matter**  2  The subject of this passage is
☐ a. witches.
☐ b. superstition.
☐ c. black cats.
☐ d. ancient beliefs. _____

**Supporting Details**  3  The Egyptian goddess Pasht had a
☐ a. woman's head and a cat's body.
☐ b. woman's head and a lion's body.
☐ c. cat's head and a man's body.
☐ d. woman's body and a cat's head. _____

**Conclusion**  4  Judging from this passage, people of the Middle Ages probably
☐ a. treated black cats with respect.
☐ b. treated black cats badly.
☐ c. were witches if they had black cats.
☐ d. thought black cats were beautiful. _____

**Clarifying Devices**  5  People of ancient Egypt and Europeans of the Middle Ages
☐ a. both worshipped black cats.
☐ b. both feared black cats.
☐ c. thought black cats could bring good luck.
☐ d. had very different feelings about black cats. _____

**Vocabulary in Context**  6  Sacred means
☐ a. dead.
☐ b. holy.
☐ c. black.
☐ d. fearful. _____

**Add your scores for questions 1–6. Enter the total here and on the graph on page 217.**  **Total Score** _____

# 59  The Badger

The badger is a member of the weasel family. It ranges throughout the western United States. It is both a help and a burden to farmers and ranchers. It kills harmful rodents, but it also digs deep holes that cause tractors to break wheels and livestock to break legs.

A clumsy critter, the slow-footed badger is built low to the ground, with short legs and a flat, squat body. It digs like a steam shovel into the rich earth of the prairie. Its strong, dark feet, each tipped with five two-inch-long nails, can dig any gopher or ground squirrel out of its burrow.

This pigeon-toed, round-shouldered ground hugger is dirty yellowish gray with a dark brown face striped with white. It may grow to more than two feet long and weigh up to twenty-five pounds. The badger has thirty-four sharp teeth and a menacing growl and hiss that make it about as sociable as a grizzly bear. Being a close cousin to the skunk, it doesn't smell very good.

An acute sense of smell enables the badger to locate food underground. It eats snakes and snails, insects, rats and mice, gophers, ground squirrels, and other rodents. Occasionally it will kill ground-nesting birds and eat their nestlings or eggs, but the badger saves many more birds than it destroys. The rodents it usually kills are animals that hunt birds. And the holes it digs in its <u>quest</u> for food provide homes for many animals.

| Main Idea | 1 | Answer | Score |
|---|---|---|---|
| | Mark the *main idea* | M | 15 |
| | Mark the statement that is *too broad* | B | 5 |
| | Mark the statement that is *too narrow* | N | 5 |

a. The slow-moving badger is considered both a help and a burden. ☐ _____

b. Prairie animals can be both helpful and harmful. ☐ _____

c. The badger hunts many rodents that live on the prairie. ☐ _____

**Score 15 points for each correct answer.** Score

**Subject Matter** **2** This passage is about
☐ a. the problems of farmers.
☐ b. the badger.
☐ c. rodents.
☐ d. prairie animals. _____

**Supporting Details** **3** According to the passage, the badger's smell
☐ a. is bad and helps to make it unsociable.
☐ b. is stronger than a skunk's smell.
☐ c. attracts rodents and snakes.
☐ d. is feared more than its sharp teeth. _____

**Conclusion** **4** The passage suggests that badgers
☐ a. are pleasant animals.
☐ b. are a nuisance to foxes and coyotes.
☐ c. aren't friendly animals.
☐ d. are lazy. _____

**Clarifying Devices** **5** The writer of this passage tells his story by depending mainly on
☐ a. cases cited by farmers and ranchers.
☐ b. logical reasoning and careful argument.
☐ c. carefully chosen descriptive words.
☐ d. facts given by scientists. _____

**Vocabulary in Context** **6** Quest means
☐ a. need.
☐ b. adventure.
☐ c. battle.
☐ d. search. _____

**Add your scores for questions 1–6. Enter the total here and on the graph on page 217.** Total Score _____

# 60 Altitude Sickness

Mountain climbing is becoming a popular sport, but it is also a potentially dangerous one. People can fall; they may also become ill from drinking bad water. One of the most common dangers to climbers is altitude sickness, an ailment that can affect even very experienced climbers.

Altitude sickness usually begins when a climber goes above 8,000 or 9,000 feet. The higher one climbs, the less oxygen there is in the air. When people don't get enough oxygen, they often begin to gasp for air. They may also feel dizzy and light-headed. Besides these common symptoms of altitude sickness, others such as nausea, headache, tiredness, and difficulty sleeping may also occur. At heights of over 18,000 feet, people may be climbing in a constant daze. This state of mind can have a serious effect on their judgment.

A few precautions can help most climbers avoid altitude sickness. The first is not to go too high too fast. If you climb to 10,000 feet, stay at that height for a day or two. Your body needs to get used to a high altitude before you climb to an even higher one. Or if you do climb higher sooner, come back down to a lower height when you sleep. Also, drink plenty of liquids and avoid tobacco and alcohol. When you reach your top height, do light activities rather than sleep too much. You breathe less when you sleep, so you get less oxygen.

The most important warning is this: if you have severe symptoms and they don't go away, go down! Don't risk injury or death because of overconfidence or lack of knowledge.

| Main Idea | 1 | | | |
|---|---|---|---|---|
| | | | Answer | Score |
| | Mark the *main idea* | | M | 15 |
| | Mark the statement that is *too broad* | | B | 5 |
| | Mark the statement that is *too narrow* | | N | 5 |
| | a. Altitude sickness is a serious ailment that can be avoided with care. | | ☐ | ___ |
| | b. Even experienced mountain climbers can get altitude sickness. | | ☐ | ___ |
| | c. Mountain climbers face many dangers. | | ☐ | ___ |

**Score 15 points for each correct answer.**                    Score

**Subject Matter**   2   This passage deals mostly with
    ☐ a. the dangers of mountain climbing.
    ☐ b. altitude sickness.
    ☐ c. protecting your lungs.
    ☐ d. avalanches.                                        _____

**Supporting**   3   The height at which climbers may begin to feel ill is
**Details**
    ☐ a. 5,000 feet.
    ☐ b. 6,000 feet.
    ☐ c. 7,000 feet.
    ☐ d. 8,000 feet.                                         _____

**Conclusion**   4   Climbing above 18,000 feet
    ☐ a. should be avoided by everyone.
    ☐ b. should not be done without a companion.
    ☐ c. will make a person think more clearly.
    ☐ d. should be the goal of all climbers.                 _____

**Clarifying**   5   The writer uses the last two paragraphs to
**Devices**
    ☐ a. describe mountain scenery.
    ☐ b. tell about a famous climber.
    ☐ c. give advice.
    ☐ d. express anger at careless climbers.                  _____

**Vocabulary**   6   Precaution means
**in Context**
    ☐ a. way of attacking a problem.
    ☐ b. care taken beforehand.
    ☐ c. objection.
    ☐ d. alternate route.                                     _____

**Add your scores for questions 1–6. Enter the total here**   Total
**and on the graph on page 217.**                             Score        _____

**121**

# 61 A Light Blazing Across the Sky

When you look up at the night sky, what do you see? There are other heavenly bodies out there besides the moon and stars. One of the most fascinating of these is a comet.

Comets were formed around the same time the Earth was formed. Usually about five to ten miles across, they are made up of ice and other frozen liquids and gases. Now and then these "dirty snowballs" begin to orbit the sun, just as the planets do. Scientists know of over one hundred comets in orbits that sometimes bring them fairly close to Earth.

As a comet gets closer to the sun, some of the gases in it begin to unfreeze. The gases combine with dust particles from the comet to form a cloud thousands of miles across. As the comet gets even nearer to the sun, a <u>solar</u> wind blows the cloud behind the comet, thus forming its tail. The tail and the generally fuzzy atmosphere around a comet are characteristics that can help you to identify this phenomenon in the night sky.

In any given year, about a dozen known comets come close to the sun in their orbits. There may also be a dozen or more newly discovered comets. The average person can't see them all, of course. Usually there are only one or two a year bright enough to be seen with the naked eye. Comet Hale-Bopp, discovered in 1995, was an unusually bright comet. Its orbit brought it relatively close to Earth—within 122 million miles of it. But Hale-Bopp came a long way on its earthly visit. It won't be back in this vicinity for another four thousand years or so.

| Main Idea | 1 | | Answer | Score |
|---|---|---|---|---|
| | Mark the *main idea* | | M | 15 |
| | Mark the statement that is *too broad* | | B | 5 |
| | Mark the statement that is *too narrow* | | N | 5 |

a. There are many heavenly bodies in the night sky. ☐ _____

b. Comets are heavenly visitors that now and then come into Earth's vicinity. ☐ _____

c. Ten or twelve comets are discovered every year. ☐ _____

**Subject Matter**  **2**  This passage is mainly about
☐ a. where comets come from.
☐ b. what comets are.
☐ c. the Hale-Bopp comet.
☐ d. how to locate comets in the night sky.  _____

**Supporting Details**  **3**  As a comet gets nearer to the sun, it
☐ a. shrinks in size.
☐ b. develops a large cloud.
☐ c. develops a small cloud.
☐ d. begins to freeze up.  _____

**Conclusion**  **4**  The phrase "dirty snowball" suggests that comets
☐ a. are very tiny.
☐ b. are pure white.
☐ c. look somewhat gray or black.
☐ d. will melt in the sun.  _____

**Clarifying Devices**  **5**  The writer develops ideas in the third paragraph by
☐ a. telling a story.
☐ b. comparing and contrasting.
☐ c. presenting a strong argument.
☐ d. explaining the steps in a process.  _____

**Vocabulary in Context**  **6**  Solar means related to the
☐ a. sun.
☐ b. moon.
☐ c. comets.
☐ d. larger planets.  _____

**Add your scores for questions 1–6. Enter the total here and on the graph on page 218.**  **Total Score**  _____

# 62 The Great Stock Market Crash

The stock market can be a wonderful place to make money. If you buy stock in a company at $12 a share and later sell it for $24, your investment has doubled. It is tempting to believe that stock prices will always increase, but they can also decrease. Prices of shares of all companies can drop simultaneously—and drop a lot. Then there is a market crash—like the one in 1929.

During the last week of October in 1929, people began to lose confidence in the market and to sell stock shares in great numbers. On October 29, the worst day, over 16 million shares of stock were traded—by far the highest number ever sold in one day. By November 13, the market temporarily bottomed out. In about three weeks it had lost 40 percent of its value, a drop of about $30 billion. It would be years before that value was regained.

What caused the crash? The 1920s had been years of tremendous growth and prosperity. Road construction skyrocketed as people traded in horses and buggies for cars. Radios and other consumer items rose in demand as more homes were wired for electricity. Feeling prosperous, many people looked to the stock market as a way to make money. Many stocks were bought on margin: put down as little as 10 percent and buy the rest on credit. Since everyone else was doing the same thing, the value of the market continued to rise. It seemed as if you couldn't lose.

When stock prices began to <u>plummet</u>, the brokers stopped giving credit and demanded to be paid the money they were owed. In a panic, people began selling everything they had. The long spiral down into the Great Depression had begun.

| Main Idea 1 | | Answer | Score |
|---|---|---|---|
| Mark the *main idea* | | M | 15 |
| Mark the statement that is *too broad* | | B | 5 |
| Mark the statement that is *too narrow* | | N | 5 |

a. The stock market crash of 1929 brought a swift end to a decade of prosperity. ☐ _____

b. The stock market can go up, but it can also go down. ☐ _____

c. Many people had begun buying on margin. ☐ _____

**Subject Matter**    **2**    This passage is mostly about
- ☐ a. the crash and the reasons for it.
- ☐ b. how people made money in the 1920s.
- ☐ c. how the stock market works.
- ☐ d. what margin is.      _____

**Supporting Details**    **3**    On the worst day of the crash, the number of shares sold was
- ☐ a. 10 million.
- ☐ b. 12 million.
- ☐ c. 16 million.
- ☐ d. 40 million.      _____

**Conclusion**    **4**    The 1920s were a decade when
- ☐ a. only rich people invested in the stock market.
- ☐ b. people with less money began to buy into the market.
- ☐ c. most people invested through stock clubs.
- ☐ d. many public warnings were given about investing too heavily in the market.      _____

**Clarifying Devices**    **5**    In this passage, the term "skyrocketed" suggests
- ☐ a. a vehicle that flies.
- ☐ b. a very fast increase.
- ☐ c. the beginning of the space program.
- ☐ d. a new way of building roads.      _____

**Vocabulary in Context**    **6**    <u>Plummet</u> means
- ☐ a. rise.
- ☐ b. go up and down rapidly.
- ☐ c. drop dramatically.
- ☐ d. dig into the earth.      _____

**Add your scores for questions 1–6. Enter the total here and on the graph on page 218.**    **Total Score**    _____

# 63 The World's Greatest Athlete?

Many people are good in one athletic event. A few excel in two. But very few can compete in a sport requiring skill in seven different events. Jackie Joyner-Kersee is someone who could. Some have called her the world's greatest athlete.

Even as a child, Jackie Joyner wanted to do well in many sports. In high school she competed in volleyball, basketball, and track. Basketball was her favorite sport then. She attended college on a four-year basketball scholarship. She became a basketball All-American.

After marrying her coach, Bob Kersee, Jackie began focusing on track. One of her best events was always the long jump. Over the years Joyner-Kersee has won many long jump medals. These include an Olympic gold medal and several world championships.

What about the sport with seven different events? It is called the heptathlon. Besides long jump, it includes events like hurdles, high jump, and shot put. Joyner-Kersee competed in this sport in four different Olympics. She won two gold medals and one silver.

Joyner-Kersee has succeeded for two reasons. Her great athletic ability is one thing. But she also possesses great mental toughness. That toughness helped her triumph in spite of her serious asthma and allergies.

Joyner-Kersee's last Olympics was in 1996. After that, she played professional basketball for a while. She did one final heptathlon in 1998 and then retired at the age of thirty-six.

| Main Idea | 1 | | Answer | Score |
|---|---|---|---|---|
| | Mark the *main idea* | | M | 15 |
| | Mark the statement that is *too broad* | | B | 5 |
| | Mark the statement that is *too narrow* | | N | 5 |

a. Only a few athletes do very well in more than one sport.  ☐  _____

b. The heptathlon is a challenging athletic event.  ☐  _____

c. Jackie Joyner-Kersee has excelled in many sports through her career.  ☐  _____

**Score 15 points for each correct answer.**                    **Score**

**Subject Matter**    **2**    The subject of this passage is
☐ a. the importance of getting into sports early in life.
☐ b. discrimination against women athletes.
☐ c. the career of Bob Kersee.
☐ d. the career of Jackie Joyner-Kersee.                    _____

**Supporting Details**    **3**    During college, Joyner-Kersee was very active in
☐ a. long jump.
☐ b. volleyball.
☐ c. basketball.
☐ d. the heptathlon.                    _____

**Conclusion**    **4**    Based on her life thus far, it would not be surprising if Joyner-Kersee
☐ a. became a referee.
☐ b. got out of sports completely.
☐ c. took up a new sport.
☐ d. became a play-by-play volleyball announcer.                    _____

**Clarifying Devices**    **5**    The passage is basically a
☐ a. biography of Jackie Joyner-Kersee.
☐ b. biography of Bob Kersee.
☐ c. history of women's sports.
☐ d. comparison between long jump and heptathlon.                    _____

**Vocabulary in Context**    **6**    In this passage, <u>triumph</u> means
☐ a. compete.
☐ b. win.
☐ c. fall in love.
☐ d. continue to smile.                    _____

**Add your scores for questions 1–6. Enter the total here and on the graph on page 218.**    **Total Score**    _____

# 64 Vipers

The family of snakes called vipers includes some of the deadliest poisonous snakes in the world. Some of the snakes in this fearsome group are the water moccasin, rattlesnake, and copperhead (all of which are found in the United States), the bushmaster and fer-de-lance of South America, and the puff adder of Africa.

Vipers have thick bodies, short tails, and triangular heads. Fangs in their upper jaws inject poison into their victims' bodies like a hypodermic needle. When the snakes bite, they contract the muscles around their poison sacs. These sacs are located behind the eyes. The poison squirts out through the hollow fangs. Almost a half-teaspoon of poison is put into a victim at one time. Fortunately, many of these snakes are small, so their bite is not fatal.

There are actually two main types of vipers—the true vipers and the pit vipers. Pit vipers live in Asia and the Americas. The name comes from a small hollow in the side of the head just below the eye. The small hollow, or pit, has a special nerve that senses heat, helping the pit viper to find its warm-blooded prey. True vipers don't have this special nerve and must rely on their <u>keen</u> sense of smell to find their food. Vipers don't usually strike unless they are disturbed or are looking for food. Still, it is a good idea to stay away from them.

| Main Idea | 1 | Answer | Score |
|---|---|---|---|
| | **Mark the *main idea*** | M | 15 |
| | **Mark the statement that is *too broad*** | B | 5 |
| | **Mark the statement that is *too narrow*** | N | 5 |
| | a. Snakes are poisonous. | ☐ | ____ |
| | b. Vipers are one of the most poisonous groups of snakes. | ☐ | ____ |
| | c. Some vipers are called pit vipers. | ☐ | ____ |

**Subject Matter**    **2**    This passage is about
☐ a. turning vipers into pets.
☐ b. how to cure snakebites.
☐ c. poisonous snakes of the world.
☐ d. vipers.          _____

**Supporting**    **3**    Which of the following is not true?
**Details**
☐ a. The bushmaster is from South America.
☐ b. Some vipers have hollows like pits.
☐ c. Pit vipers are found in Africa.
☐ d. A viper's fangs are hollow.          _____

**Conclusion**    **4**    We can infer from the passage that
☐ a. all snakes with triangular heads are vipers.
☐ b. small vipers are harmless because of small amounts of venom.
☐ c. very long snakes are not vipers.
☐ d. when snakes are extremely hungry they eat people.          _____

**Clarifying**    **5**    The author compares the viper's poison-injecting
**Devices**          fangs to
☐ a. a squirt gun.
☐ b. a hypodermic needle.
☐ c. triangular needles.
☐ d. biting machines.          _____

**Vocabulary**    **6**    The word <u>keen</u> means
**in Context**
☐ a. really nice.
☐ b. eager.
☐ c. vivid.
☐ d. very sensitive.          _____

**Add your scores for questions 1–6. Enter the total here**    **Total**
**and on the graph on page 218.**    **Score**          _____

# 65 The Black Death

Imagine an illness so serious that people might go to bed well and be dead before morning. Think of this illness striking most of your family and friends. How would you respond? This question faced many Europeans in the 1300s as bubonic plague—the Black Death—swept the continent.

The plague <u>rampaged</u> across Europe beginning in late 1347. Its symptoms were terrible. In one form, sufferers developed egg-sized black swellings in their armpits and groins. These swellings were followed by boils and strange black blotches on their skin, the result of internal bleeding. In another form of the disease swellings didn't develop, but people spit blood instead. In both forms, people contracted a severe fever, and they were dead within hours or days.

The plague was spread either by contact with blood or by respiratory infection. The respiratory infection meant that if a person coughed on you, you could get the disease. And if you got it, you most probably died. By the time the plague burned itself out in 1350, over twenty million Europeans had died from it. The city of Paris lost half of its population; Venice lost about two-thirds. Sufferers died so fast that there often wasn't time to bury them, and bodies piled up in the streets. The plague was responsible for a decades-long shortage of people.

Today an outbreak of plague could be controlled with antibiotics, but no such cure existed 650 years ago. Many escaped the only way they could: by deserting sick friends and families. A few got to isolated areas where the plague had not hit, but most did not—and died anyway.

| Main Idea | 1 | Answer | Score |
|---|---|---|---|
| | Mark the *main idea* | M | 15 |
| | Mark the statement that is *too broad* | B | 5 |
| | Mark the statement that is *too narrow* | N | 5 |

a. The Black Plague raced across Europe, killing great numbers of people. ☐ _____

b. Many large cities lost large portions of the population during the Black Plague. ☐ _____

c. People have always feared infectious diseases. ☐ _____

**Score 15 points for each correct answer.**     **Score**

Subject Matter   2   This passage is mainly about
☐ a. the Black Plague and the destruction it caused.
☐ b. how people got the plague.
☐ c. how plague could be controlled now.
☐ d. diseases that are quick killers.             _____

Supporting   3   A characteristic of both forms of plague was
Details           ☐ a. boils.
☐ b. spitting blood.
☐ c. severe fever.
☐ d. egg-shaped black swellings.               _____

Conclusion   4   The final paragraph suggests that people
☐ a. cared for their loved ones as long as they could.
☐ b. wanted to protect their children.
☐ c. were frightened and selfish.
☐ d. had a good understanding of how plague spread.       _____

Clarifying   5   The expression "the plague burned itself out"
Devices          means that the plague
☐ a. self-destructed.
☐ b. set people on fire.
☐ c. traveled as fast as a blazing fire.
☐ d. could not be controlled.                  _____

Vocabulary   6   Rampaged means
in Context        ☐ a. moved slowly and cautiously.
☐ b. rushed wildly.
☐ c. traveled.
☐ d. slept.                           _____

**Add your scores for questions 1–6. Enter the total here     Total
and on the graph on page 218.                    Score     _____**

# 66 The Man from Stratford

What makes a person famous? This is a mystery that many people have pondered. All kinds of myths surround the lives of well-known people.

Most people are familiar with the works of William Shakespeare, one of the greatest English writers of the sixteenth and seventeenth centuries. Yet how many know Shakespeare the person, the man behind the works?

After centuries of research, scholars are still trying to discover Shakespeare's personal history. It is not easily found in his writings. Authors of the time could not protect their works. An acting company, for example, could change a play if they wanted to. Nowadays writers have copyrights that protect their work.

Many myths arose about Shakespeare. Some said he had no <u>formal</u> education. Others believe that he began his career by tending the horses of wealthy men.

All of these myths are interesting, but are they true? Probably not. Shakespeare's father was a respected man in Stratford, a member of the town council. He sent young William to grammar school. Most people of Elizabethan times did not continue beyond grammar school, so Shakespeare did have at least an average education.

Some parts of Shakespeare's life will always remain unknown. The Great London Fire of 1666 burned many important documents that could have been a source of clues. We will always be left with many questions and few facts.

| Main Idea 1 | | Answer | Score |
|---|---|---|---|
| Mark the *main idea* | | M | 15 |
| Mark the statement that is *too broad* | | B | 5 |
| Mark the statement that is *too narrow* | | N | 5 |

|   |   |   |   |
|---|---|---|---|
| a. | Very little is known about Shakespeare as a person. | ☐ | _____ |
| b. | Shakespeare's writings are all we have as clues about him. | ☐ | _____ |
| c. | The background of many sixteenth-century writers is a mystery. | ☐ | _____ |

**Score 15 points for each correct answer.**

**Subject Matter**    **2**    This passage deals with

☐ a. the Great London Fire.

☐ b. the lost documents of Shakespeare.

☐ c. scholars of Shakespeare.

☐ d. Shakespeare's personal history.      _____

**Supporting Details**    **3**    Parts of Shakespeare's life continue to remain a mystery because

☐ a. people are not interested.

☐ b. researchers do not have the expertise to find the facts.

☐ c. writers had no claim over their works.

☐ d. the Great London Fire burned important documents.      _____

**Conclusion**    **4**    From this passage we can infer that Shakespeare

☐ a. was a horse thief.

☐ b. had no education.

☐ c. is surrounded by myths.

☐ d. was popular in Stratford.      _____

**Clarifying Devices**    **5**    The first sentence arouses interest by presenting

☐ a. a direct statement.

☐ b. a question.

☐ c. an emotional appeal.

☐ d. a contrast.      _____

**Vocabulary in Context**    **6**    In this passage formal means

☐ a. correct.

☐ b. organized.

☐ c. rigid.

☐ d. elaborate.      _____

**Add your scores for questions 1–6. Enter the total here and on the graph on page 218.**    **Total Score**      _____

# 67 Once Poison, Now a Food

Would you eat a bacon, lettuce, and love apple sandwich? You probably have eaten many of them. Love apple was the name used many years ago for the tomato.

The tomato was originally an American plant. It was found in South America by early Spanish explorers. The word *tomato* comes from the native Nahuatl word *tomatl*. But when it moved north, the plant earned a different name. Remarkably, the settlers in North America thought it was poisonous. They believed that to eat it was surely to die. It was said that jilted <u>suitors</u> would threaten to eat a tomato to cause their cold-hearted lovers remorse. Because of this legend, the settlers called the tomato a "love apple." While people enjoyed other native plants, such as corn and sweet potatoes, everyone avoided the tomato.

No one knows who first dared to eat a tomato. Perhaps someone was brave enough, or lovesick enough, to try out the truth of the rumors. Of course, whoever ate this fruit was perfectly safe. No one died from eating a love apple. Still, it was many years before the people fully believed that the tomato was a safe, and even good, food. But its use did become common, and the plant was sent across the ocean to become part of many traditional European dishes.

| Main Idea | 1 | | |
|---|---|---|---|
| | | **Answer** | **Score** |
| | Mark the *main idea* | M | 15 |
| | Mark the statement that is *too broad* | B | 5 |
| | Mark the statement that is *too narrow* | N | 5 |

a. Many foods have legends associated with them. ☐ _____

b. Although the tomato was thought to be poisonous, no one died from eating it. ☐ _____

c. Long ago the tomato was called a "love apple" and was thought to be poisonous. ☐ _____

**Subject Matter**  **2**  Another good title for this passage would be
- [ ] a. Life in Early America.
- [ ] b. What Happens to the Brokenhearted.
- [ ] c. The History of the Tomato.
- [ ] d. Vegetables in Our Diet.  _____

**Supporting Details**  **3**  The language from which we derived the word *tomato* is
- [ ] a. Portuguese.
- [ ] b. Spanish.
- [ ] c. Nahuatl.
- [ ] d. European.  _____

**Conclusion**  **4**  The origin of the story about tomatoes being poisonous is
- [ ] a. South America.
- [ ] b. jilted lovers.
- [ ] c. an early settler who ate a tomato and got ill.
- [ ] d. unknown.  _____

**Clarifying Devices**  **5**  The word "still" in the middle of the third paragraph tells you that
- [ ] a. people continued to be wary of tomatoes.
- [ ] b. people became very quiet when speaking of tomatoes.
- [ ] c. the writer is pointing out similarities.
- [ ] d. the writer is not sure about the truth of the following statement.  _____

**Vocabulary in Context**  **6**  Suitor means
- [ ] a. boyfriend or girlfriend.
- [ ] b. launderer.
- [ ] c. tailor.
- [ ] d. explorer.  _____

**Add your scores for questions 1–6. Enter the total here and on the graph on page 218.**    **Total Score**  _____

# 68 Developing the Desktop Computer

Can you remember a time without computers? Large computers have been around for many years. But small ones, the desktop kind, are a fairly new invention.

Two people who helped make small computers popular are Steven Jobs and Stephen Wozniak. The two technology buffs began designing their first computer in Jobs's bedroom. (They actually built it in Jobs's parents' garage.) That computer was the Apple I, and it was mostly a toy. The next year, 1977, they put out the Apple II. It was the first easy-to-use desktop computer and became a huge seller.

Apple Computer, Inc., took the computer world by storm. IBM, which made big computers, did not even enter the desktop computer market until several years later.

In 1984 Apple introduced their latest <u>innovation</u>: the Macintosh. Like the Apple II, it was an easy-to-use computer. It was the first computer to show icons such as the "Trash" container on the screen. It was the first popular computer to use a mouse. The icons and the mouse made it easy to do things like move and save files. A person could work without memorizing a lot of confusing keyboard commands.

Wozniak and Jobs didn't stay with the company they founded. And as time went on, the company was less successful. But their new ideas changed computer use. They were instrumental in bringing the Computer Age into people's businesses and homes.

| Main Idea | 1 | | Answer | Score |
|---|---|---|---|---|
| | **Mark the _main idea_** | | **M** | 15 |
| | **Mark the statement that is _too broad_** | | **B** | 5 |
| | **Mark the statement that is _too narrow_** | | **N** | 5 |

a. Steven Jobs and Stephen Wozniak developed several important early desktop computers. ☐ _____

b. Jobs and Wozniak beat out IBM by several years. ☐ _____

c. The invention of desktop computers changed the way business is done. ☐ _____

**Score 15 points for each correct answer.**          **Score**

**Subject Matter**      **2**    Another good title for this selection would be
- [ ] a. The Beginnings of Apple Computer.
- [ ] b. Building Computers Cheaply.
- [ ] c. The Macintosh.
- [ ] d. Success and Failure.          _____

**Supporting Details**      **3**    Jobs and Wozniak's first computer was built
- [ ] a. for $700.
- [ ] b. in Jobs's bedroom.
- [ ] c. in Jobs's parents' garage.
- [ ] d. at Apple Computer.          _____

**Conclusion**      **4**    It is safe to assume that
- [ ] a. Jobs and Wozniak did not take their ideas too seriously.
- [ ] b. Apple Computers are no longer easy to use.
- [ ] c. few people had desktop computers before the late 1970s.
- [ ] d. IBM always realized the importance of desktop computers.          _____

**Clarifying Devices**      **5**    The information in this passage is presented in
- [ ] a. chronological order.
- [ ] b. cause and effect order.
- [ ] c. spatial order.
- [ ] d. order of importance.          _____

**Vocabulary in Context**      **6**    An <u>innovation</u> is a(n)
- [ ] a. new idea or thing.
- [ ] b. keyboard.
- [ ] c. mouse.
- [ ] d. idea recycled from the past.          _____

**Add your scores for questions 1–6. Enter the total here and on the graph on page 218.**     Total Score          _____

# 69 A Dish Fit for Royalty

When people think of caviar, they think of elegant parties given by wealthy people. Actually, not all caviar is terribly costly; you sometimes find domestic—home-grown—caviar on buffet tables in all-you-can-eat restaurants. But the best kinds of caviar are very expensive indeed.

Caviar is fish eggs. The top variety comes from three kinds of sturgeons found in the Caspian Sea in Russia: beluga, osetra, and sevruga. These fish take between nine and fifteen years to mature and produce eggs. When they do, they generally yield a few pounds of tiny, dark brown or dark gray eggs apiece. The scarcity of caviar and the long time it takes to harvest are what make caviar expensive. One *ounce* of beluga can cost around $50 to $60 in a retail store.

Why do people eat caviar? Some, naturally, are <u>entranced</u> by anything so expensive. But there are also people who appreciate the taste. Beluga is said to have a creamy, buttery taste. Osetra has a nutty flavor. True fans will eat top-quality caviar by itself on dry toast points; the fat from the eggs will moisten the bread.

If you've never tried caviar, you might want to see what an inexpensive type tastes like. Caviar from North American sturgeon costs less than a third as much as the most expensive Russian types. Some people also call salmon eggs caviar. These slightly larger, bright red eggs are the least expensive of all. If you're in doubt, go to the nearest fish buffet and see if you can sample them there!

| Main Idea | 1 | Answer | Score |
|---|---|---|---|
| | Mark the *main idea* | M | 15 |
| | Mark the statement that is *too broad* | B | 5 |
| | Mark the statement that is *too narrow* | N | 5 |
| | a. Rare foods are expensive. | ☐ | _____ |
| | b. Rare and expensive, caviar is a delicacy many people like. | ☐ | _____ |
| | c. Three kinds of sturgeons produce Russian caviar. | ☐ | _____ |

**Subject Matter**   **2**   This selection is about

☐ a. fishing for sturgeon.

☐ b. harvesting and eating caviar.

☐ c. the differences between Russian and American caviar.

☐ d. the colors of fish eggs.     _____

**Supporting Details**   **3**   Caviar is scarce because

☐ a. it takes a long time for a small amount to develop.

☐ b. no one is willing to harvest it.

☐ c. local fishermen eat the sturgeon and throw away the eggs.

☐ d. the waters where sturgeon are found are polluted.     _____

**Conclusion**   **4**   The writer's attitude seems to be

☐ a. only expensive caviar is good.

☐ b. keep an open mind about eating caviar.

☐ c. people who eat caviar are snobs.

☐ d. don't buy caviar at retail prices.     _____

**Clarifying Devices**   **5**   The writer mentions "beluga, osetra, and sevruga" to

☐ a. explain places where caviar is found.

☐ b. identify three types of Russian caviar.

☐ c. list companies that sell caviar.

☐ d. mention famous Russians who enjoyed caviar.     _____

**Vocabulary in Context**   **6**   Entranced, as used in this passage, means

☐ a. surprised.

☐ b. alarmed.

☐ c. disgusted.

☐ d. charmed or delighted.     _____

**Add your scores for questions 1–6. Enter the total here and on the graph on page 218.**     **Total Score**     _____

# 70 Asteroids and Meteorites

In addition to comets, two other relatively small bodies can be found floating around the solar system. They are known as asteroids and meteorites. Asteroids are smallish bodies that orbit the sun, mainly in the area between Mars and Jupiter. Though not large enough to be thought of as planets, asteroids can range from the size of a small boulder to several hundred miles in diameter. They are rocky bodies made up of various metals and other substances. Now and then something will jar an asteroid out of its orbit. Then it may approach or—very rarely—hit Earth.

Meteorites are also small, rocky bodies that have traveled through space. Some may be broken-off pieces of asteroids; some may be leftover chunks of comets. Meteorites are pieces of rock from space that actually hit our planet.

When these intruders make contact, what damage do they do? It all depends on their size and where they hit. Since Earth is mostly made up of water, a small meteorite falling into the Atlantic Ocean probably won't harm anything. But some meteorites strike solid ground. A meteorite weighing about sixty tons once hit near a farm in southern Africa. Another huge one broke up in the air above Siberia in 1908. It destroyed trees in a twenty-mile area.

The damage from a huge fallen asteroid can be far worse. In eastern Mexico are the remains of a basin one hundred miles wide where an asteroid touched Earth 65 million years ago. Enough <u>debris</u> shot forth to block out the sun's light for decades. When there was light again, all the dinosaurs had disappeared.

**Main Idea**    1

|  | Answer | Score |
|---|---|---|
| Mark the *main idea* | M | 15 |
| Mark the statement that is *too broad* | B | 5 |
| Mark the statement that is *too narrow* | N | 5 |

a. Asteroids and meteorites hit Earth and sometimes do damage. ☐ _____

b. A meteorite can weigh as much as sixty tons. ☐ _____

c. Asteroids and meteorites float around the solar system. ☐ _____

**Subject Matter** 2 This passage deals mostly with
- [ ] a. the history of asteroids and meteorites.
- [ ] b. what happens when asteroids and meteorites hit Earth.
- [ ] c. comparing asteroids and meteorites.
- [ ] d. the destruction of the dinosaurs.

_____

**Supporting Details** 3 Asteroids and meteorites are similar in that
- [ ] a. both are broken-off pieces of comets.
- [ ] b. both are rocky bodies.
- [ ] c. they orbit the sun in the area of Mars and Jupiter.
- [ ] d. neither can be more than about a mile wide.

_____

**Conclusion** 4 The most likely reason for the dinosaurs' disappearance is that
- [ ] a. their eyesight couldn't adapt to the dark.
- [ ] b. without sunlight, plants and other foods were no longer available.
- [ ] c. people began to inhabit the planet.
- [ ] d. the asteroid hit caused the land to flood.

_____

**Clarifying Devices** 5 In paragraph 3, the phrase "these intruders" refers to
- [ ] a. dinosaurs.
- [ ] b. comets.
- [ ] c. asteroids and meteorites.
- [ ] d. human beings.

_____

**Vocabulary in Context** 6 Debris in this passage means
- [ ] a. dinosaur remains.
- [ ] b. frozen water.
- [ ] c. fragments of rock.
- [ ] d. garbage.

_____

**Add your scores for questions 1–6. Enter the total here and on the graph on page 218.**

**Total Score**

_____

# 71 El Niño

When you live in an area for a while, you get used to its climate. You know about how cold and wet it will be in March and how warm in August. Sometimes, though, weather conditions occur that create big changes in temperature and rainfall. One of these is called El Niño.

In an El Niño situation the surface water in the eastern Pacific Ocean, near the coast of Peru, gets unusually warm. (This warming occurs around Christmas; "El Niño" is Spanish for "Christ Child.") Rainfall seems to follow the warm water, so that areas around Peru get floods. But the weather change doesn't stop there. Regions to the west of the warm water, such as Australia, get very little rain and so experience drought. El Niño also influences the United States. Usually California gets very severe rains. The middle and eastern parts of the country have winters that are much warmer than normal.

El Niños have been occurring for hundreds of years, but people didn't understand what was happening. It was only in the 1960s that scientists found definite proof that warming in the Pacific affected weather elsewhere. Computers are continuing to <u>compile</u> information about how an El Niño works. We know, for instance, that the condition occurs every two to seven years. Usually it lasts for several months, though sometimes it can last for years. And its effects can vary: some El Niños are much stronger than others. Often an El Niño year is followed by one with a condition called La Niña. In this situation, the Pacific waters get very cold and the weather patterns of El Niño tend to be reversed.

| Main Idea | 1 | | |
|---|---|---|---|
| | | **Answer** | **Score** |
| | Mark the *main idea* | M | 15 |
| | Mark the statement that is *too broad* | B | 5 |
| | Mark the statement that is *too narrow* | N | 5 |

a. El Niño is named for the Christ Child. ☐ _____

b. Many conditions can affect weather. ☐ _____

c. An El Niño situation causes dramatic weather changes. ☐ _____

**Subject Matter**     **2**  Another good title for this selection would be
- [ ] a. El Niño and La Niña.
- [ ] b. A Cold Ocean Situation.
- [ ] c. A Real Drought Maker.
- [ ] d. Turning the Weather Upside Down.

_____

**Supporting Details**     **3**  In an El Niño situation, regions around Peru get
- [ ] a. snow.
- [ ] b. drought.
- [ ] c. violent winds.
- [ ] d. floods.

_____

**Conclusion**     **4**  During La Niña, the weather in California is most likely very
- [ ] a. dry.
- [ ] b. wet.
- [ ] c. cold.
- [ ] d. warm.

_____

**Clarifying Devices**     **5**  The author begins this passage by
- [ ] a. referring to weather patterns readers are already familiar with.
- [ ] b. defining El Niño.
- [ ] c. talking about Pacific Ocean water.
- [ ] d. telling an interesting story.

_____

**Vocabulary in Context**     **6**  Compile means
- [ ] a. hide.
- [ ] b. notice.
- [ ] c. write about.
- [ ] d. collect.

_____

**Add your scores for questions 1–6. Enter the total here and on the graph on page 218.**     **Total Score**

_____

# 72 The Witch's Wind

In California it's called the "Santa Ana." Argentineans call it the "zonda." It has more than twenty other local names; one of the most fitting is the "witch's wind." The scientific name of this mysterious wind is *foehn,* pronounced fern.

A foehn is a moving mass of air that, after crossing mountains, becomes a dry, gusty wind that moves with great power. A witch's wind in Texas once flattened 252 oil derricks. One in Austria derailed three streetcars, each weighing over three tons.

There is an unresolved mystery in the witch's wind. The foehn can have a strange and hard-to-explain effect on people's physical and mental <u>states</u>. When the wind is blowing, some people experience what in Europe is called "the foehn disease." Those who suffer from it say they are depressed and can't concentrate. In Germany, you can even buy anti-foehn pills.

In many places, there have been increases in the numbers of accidents, suicides, and calls for medical help during the wind. The foehn has been blamed for everything from drops in factory production to family quarrels. In California during the 1890s, people who committed crimes of passion during the witch's wind could use the foehn as an excuse.

Some people feel symptoms even before the wind arrives. They may have headaches or breathing problems. Their skin becomes taut, and old scars ache. These signs have occurred in people as much as ten hours before scientific weather equipment detected the foehn's approach.

| Main Idea | 1 | Answer | Score |
|---|---|---|---|
| | Mark the *main idea* | M | 15 |
| | Mark the statement that is *too broad* | B | 5 |
| | Mark the statement that is *too narrow* | N | 5 |

a. The witch's wind is a strong wind with a mysterious effect on people. ☐ _____

b. The witch's wind has great destructive force. ☐ _____

c. Weather changes can produce mysterious mental effects. ☐ _____

**Subject Matter**    **2**    The passage is mainly about
- ☐ a. the destructive power of wind.
- ☐ b. different types of winds.
- ☐ c. how weather affects people.
- ☐ d. foehns.    _____

**Supporting Details**    **3**    The foehn is mysterious because
- ☐ a. of its power to lift great weights.
- ☐ b. its origin is unknown.
- ☐ c. it can affect physical and mental health.
- ☐ d. it occurs in many different areas of the world.    _____

**Conclusion**    **4**    The passage implies that "witch's wind" is a good name for the foehn because
- ☐ a. the word foehn means "witch."
- ☐ b. it has a strange and harmful power.
- ☐ c. it causes depression.
- ☐ d. it has become legendary.    _____

**Clarifying Devices**    **5**    The writer tells how the foehn "flattened 252 oil derricks" in order to
- ☐ a. impress the reader with the wind's power.
- ☐ b. explain the mystery of the foehn.
- ☐ c. emphasize how unpredictable the wind is.
- ☐ d. compare the foehn with other destructive natural forces.    _____

**Vocabulary in Context**    **6**    As used in the passage, the word <u>states</u> means
- ☐ a. positions.
- ☐ b. declares.
- ☐ c. nations.
- ☐ d. conditions.    _____

**Add your scores for questions 1–6. Enter the total here and on the graph on page 218.**     **Total Score**     _____

# 73 A Fighter for Justice

He was denied admission to one law school because he was black. But today that same school has a law library named after him. You may not know much about Thurgood Marshall, but he strengthened education rights for African Americans all over the country.

Marshall was born in Baltimore in 1908. Like other African American students of his time, he went to <u>segregated</u> schools. These schools were not illegal. An 1896 law stated that schools for blacks and whites could be "separate but equal." But Marshall knew that most black schools were not equal. He decided to do something about it.

Marshall received a law degree from Howard University. Then he began to work at changing the country's schools. Marshall's strategy was to start with colleges and graduate schools, because he thought judges would sympathize with ambitious young African Americans searching for an education. In 1935, he successfully sued the University of Maryland Law School to accept its first black student. Other cases followed, with similar results.

By the 1950s, Marshall was ready to turn to grade schools and high schools. In 1954, he accepted the case of Linda Brown, who wanted to attend a white grade school near her home. As a result of Marshall's arguments, the Supreme Court changed the law. It said that "separate" schools could never be "equal."

In 1967, Marshall became the first African American appointed to the U.S. Supreme Court. Until he retired in 1991, he supported many other civil rights bills.

| Main Idea | 1 | | Answer | Score |
|---|---|---|---|---|
| | Mark the *main idea* | | M | 15 |
| | Mark the statement that is *too broad* | | B | 5 |
| | Mark the statement that is *too narrow* | | N | 5 |

|  |  |  |  |
|---|---|---|---|
| a. | Thurgood Marshall took on the case of student Linda Brown. | ☐ | _____ |
| b. | The Supreme Court frequently rules on racial issues. | ☐ | _____ |
| c. | Thurgood Marshall was responsible for changing the "separate but equal" law. | ☐ | _____ |

**Subject Matter**    **2**    This passage is basically about
- ☐ a. Thurgood Marshall's childhood.
- ☐ b. Thurgood Marshall's influence on American education.
- ☐ c. Thurgood Marshall on the Supreme Court.
- ☐ d. inequality in America.

**Supporting Details**    **3**    The first schools that Marshall tried to change were
- ☐ a. public elementary schools.
- ☐ b. public high schools.
- ☐ c. private schools.
- ☐ d. colleges.

**Conclusion**    **4**    As a lawyer, Marshall must have been very
- ☐ a. cruel.
- ☐ b. easygoing.
- ☐ c. persuasive.
- ☐ d. confusing.

**Clarifying Devices**    **5**    The first two sentences of this passage
- ☐ a. set up a contrast.
- ☐ b. are intended to criticize.
- ☐ c. give the steps in a process.
- ☐ d. explain basic facts about Marshall's childhood.

**Vocabulary in Context**    **6**    <u>Segregated</u> in this passage means
- ☐ a. good.
- ☐ b. locally run.
- ☐ c. separated by race.
- ☐ d. poor.

**Add your scores for questions 1–6. Enter the total here and on the graph on page 218.**    **Total Score**    _____

# 74 What Makes a Dynasty?

Sports fans love to discuss dynasties—teams that did so well for so long that while they were successful they seemed almost to own their sport. They don't necessarily have to win the World Series or Super Bowl or NBA title every single year. But in those few years they don't win, they must come pretty close.

Who were some of the great sports dynasties? Certainly the New York Yankees in the 1920s, when Babe Ruth was playing. (The Yankees also had a dynasty in the '50s and '60s, with stars like Yogi Berra and Mickey Mantle.) There were also the Boston Celtics, who <u>dominated</u> professional basketball from the late 1950s all the way through the '60s, and the Chicago Bulls, who owned the sport in the 1990s. The Green Bay Packers pretty much dominated football in the '60s, in the Vince Lombardi years. In hockey, the Montreal Canadiens were the team to beat through much of the '50s, '60s, and '70s.

Beyond that, calling any team a dynasty gets a little dicey. For instance, Pittsburgh, Dallas, and San Francisco have each played in, and won, several Super Bowls. But have any of these teams dominated football for an extended period? Do the New York Islanders' four consecutive Stanley Cups in the early 1980s make them a hockey dynasty for that period? Questions like these don't have hard and fast answers. What you think depends, to a large extent, on where you live and which teams you support. But that is what makes sports interesting.

**Main Idea** 1

|  | Answer | Score |
|---|---|---|
| Mark the *main idea* | M | 15 |
| Mark the statement that is *too broad* | B | 5 |
| Mark the statement that is *too narrow* | N | 5 |

a. A dynasty can happen in any sport. ☐ _____

b. Only a few teams are strong enough to be called dynasties. ☐ _____

c. The Boston Celtics were a very strong basketball team. ☐ _____

**Subject Matter**    **2**    Another good title for this selection would be
- ☐ a. Which Football Teams Qualify?
- ☐ b. Only the Very Best.
- ☐ c. Who Will Be Next?
- ☐ d. The Death of Sports Dynasties.                    _____

**Supporting Details**    **3**    The coach of the Green Bay Packer dynasty was
- ☐ a. Yogi Berra.
- ☐ b. Bart Starr.
- ☐ c. Vince Lombardi.
- ☐ d. Mike Holmgren.                    _____

**Conclusion**    **4**    The writer believes that
- ☐ a. there can be no agreement on which teams are dynasties.
- ☐ b. dynasties have some identifiable characteristics.
- ☐ c. hometown fans are very biased.
- ☐ d. there will be no dynasties beyond the 1990s.    _____

**Clarifying Devices**    **5**    In the course of this passage the writer
- ☐ a. asks several questions and answers all of them.
- ☐ b. asks several questions and answers some of them.
- ☐ c. asks no questions.
- ☐ d. mentions that only fans have sports questions.    _____

**Vocabulary in Context**    **6**    Dominated means
- ☐ a. bossed.
- ☐ b. held home court advantage in.
- ☐ c. had winning records in.
- ☐ d. controlled by strength or power.                    _____

**Add your scores for questions 1–6. Enter the total here**    **Total**
**and on the graph on page 218.**    **Score**    _____

# 75 A Leader of Her Country

By the 1990s, people had become accustomed to seeing women in high government posts. People were not so accustomed to this in the 1960s, however. Yet that is when Golda Meir became prime minister of Israel.

Meir was born in the Ukraine. However, she emigrated to the United States with her family as a young child. She grew up in Milwaukee, where her mother ran a grocery store. Meir trained to be a schoolteacher and married when she was about twenty.

As a young woman, Meir heard stories of the struggles to establish a Jewish homeland. In 1921, she and her husband moved to Palestine to work with the Jewish groups there. She was <u>instrumental</u> in helping Israel become an independent state in 1948. When the new government was formed, Meir was the only woman to belong to the provisional council of state, the legislative part of the government. She took an active role in establishing policy.

In 1969, the Israeli prime minister died suddenly, and Meir was chosen as a compromise candidate for the position. She remained prime minister until 1974.

Seventy-one years old when she took office, Meir was a plain-looking, plain-dressing woman. She reminded some people of a kindly grandmother. But it was a mistake to underestimate her strength and will. She led her country through peace and war. After her death in 1978, Meir was called "one of the great women in Jewish and world history."

**Main Idea** 1

| | Answer | Score |
|---|---|---|
| **Mark the *main idea*** | M | 15 |
| **Mark the statement that is *too broad*** | B | 5 |
| **Mark the statement that is *too narrow*** | N | 5 |

a. Few women have become leaders of countries. ☐ _____

b. Golda Meir worked for a Jewish homeland for most of her life. ☐ _____

c. Israel became an independent state in 1948. ☐ _____

**Subject Matter**  **2**  The subject of this passage is
☐ a. the career of Golda Meir.
☐ b. how people learn to accept responsibility.
☐ c. discrimination against women leaders.
☐ d. remaining active even when elderly.          _____

**Supporting Details**  **3**  Golda Meir became prime minister
☐ a. right after Israel won independence.
☐ b. by winning a landslide election.
☐ c. as a compromise candidate.
☐ d. but was quickly pushed out of power.          _____

**Conclusion**  **4**  When Israel became a state, the people in power
☐ a. were mostly young.
☐ b. had a lot of experience running a country.
☐ c. were an equal mix of men and women.
☐ d. included few women.          _____

**Clarifying Devices**  **5**  The passage is basically a
☐ a. biography of Golda Meir.
☐ b. history of Israel.
☐ c. discussion of emigration.
☐ d. description of life in Milwaukee.          _____

**Vocabulary in Context**  **6**  In this passage, <u>instrumental</u> means
☐ a. musical.
☐ b. very helpful.
☐ c. useless.
☐ d. recognized.          _____

**Add your scores for questions 1–6. Enter the total here**  Total
**and on the graph on page 218.**  Score          _____

# 76  A Maker of Mobiles

You probably know what a mobile is. These delicate constructions, hanging from the ceiling and moving gently with every breeze, delight both children and adults. But do you know who invented the mobile? This lovely creation was the work of an American artist named Alexander Calder.

Calder became interested in making things when he was a child, and even then he often used wire in his constructions. When he went to college, he studied engineering rather than art. But he quickly realized that art was his real passion. He also loved the circus, and many of his early art works were small circus figures made with wire and a pliers.

In about 1930, Calder turned from realistic wire figures to <u>abstract</u> ones. He began constructing objects that had circles, squares, and other geometric shapes intersecting each other. To get the shapes to move, he used small motors or hand cranks. Then he went one step beyond these early mobiles. He got the shapes in his constructions to move by themselves.

A mobile may look simple as it shifts in the wind, but it requires careful construction to work properly. Calder used his engineering knowledge to create his first mobiles. Often these consisted of small pieces of brightly painted metal strung by wire to a thicker base wire. Calder learned how to find the precise point to connect each wire so that all the pieces would sway in harmony. In doing so, he created an art form for people all over the world to copy and enjoy.

| Main Idea | 1 | | |
|---|---|---|---|
| | | Answer | Score |
| | Mark the *main idea* | M | 15 |
| | Mark the statement that is *too broad* | B | 5 |
| | Mark the statement that is *too narrow* | N | 5 |

a. Mobile are creations that move in the wind. ☐ _____

b. Alexander Calder's experiments with wire led to the first mobiles. ☐ _____

c. Calder was always interested in the circus. ☐ _____

**Score 15 points for each correct answer.**          **Score**

**Subject Matter**     2    The subject of this passage is
- [ ] a. mobiles around the world.
- [ ] b. how Calder came to develop the mobile.
- [ ] c. how mobiles are made.
- [ ] d. Calder's early art education.

_____

**Supporting Details**     3    Many of Calder's early art works were
- [ ] a. mobiles.
- [ ] b. circles and triangles.
- [ ] c. large sculptures.
- [ ] d. wire circus figures.

_____

**Conclusion**     4    Based on his work, Calder seemed to have a personality that was
- [ ] a. bitter.
- [ ] b. serious.
- [ ] c. playful.
- [ ] d. egotistical.

_____

**Clarifying Devices**     5    Alliteration is the use of words with the same beginning consonant. Which of the following uses alliteration?
- [ ] a. "an American artist"
- [ ] b. "A Maker of Mobiles"
- [ ] c. "pieces of brightly painted metal"
- [ ] d. "engineering rather than art"

_____

**Vocabulary in Context**     6    As used in this passage, the word <u>abstract</u> means
- [ ] a. not looking like realistic people or objects.
- [ ] b. hard to visualize.
- [ ] c. geometric.
- [ ] d. made of wire.

_____

**Add your scores for questions 1–6. Enter the total here and on the graph on page 218.**          **Total Score**

_____

# 77 Fire Is Fearsome

People often speak of fire as though it were a living creature—it grows, dances, needs oxygen, feeds on whatever it can find, and then dies. And when a forest fire rages out of control, threatening human lives and homes, it must be fought like a "wild animal." The fight is often desperate, since firefighters' best efforts may be dwarfed by the fury of a large fire. But the fire's own traits can be used against it.

The heated air above a fire rises in a pillar of smoke and burnt gases, pulling fresh air in from the sides to replace it. Firefighters use this fact when they "fight fire with fire." They start a fire well in front of the one that they are fighting. Instead of traveling on in front of the inferno, the smaller fire is pulled back toward it by the updrafts of the larger blaze. As it travels back to meet the large fire, the smaller backfire burns away the fuel that the forest fire needs to survive.

Even when a backfire has been well set, however, the fire may still win the struggle. The wind that the firefighters used to help them may now become their enemy. When the backfire meets the main fire, before both die for lack of fuel, there is tremendous flame, great heat, and <u>turbulent</u> winds. A strong gust may blow the fire into the treetops beyond the area, giving the fire new fuel and a new life.

| Main Idea | 1 | | Answer | Score |
|---|---|---|---|---|
| | **Mark the _main idea_** | | M | 15 |
| | **Mark the statement that is _too broad_** | | B | 5 |
| | **Mark the statement that is _too narrow_** | | N | 5 |
| | a. A fire's own characteristics can be used to fight it. | | ☐ | _____ |
| | b. Backfires are used to "fight fire with fire." | | ☐ | _____ |
| | c. Fire can be useful as well as dangerous. | | ☐ | _____ |

**Subject Matter**   2   This passage focuses on
- [ ] a. how fires start.
- [ ] b. damage caused by fire.
- [ ] c. the fascination of fire.
- [ ] d. fighting forest fires.

_____

**Supporting Details**   3   A backfire is started
- [ ] a. behind a forest fire.
- [ ] b. ahead of a forest fire.
- [ ] c. on the sides of a forest fire.
- [ ] d. all around a forest fire.

_____

**Conclusion**   4   This passage suggests that a fire will travel
- [ ] a. faster than a horse can run.
- [ ] b. in all directions at the same speed.
- [ ] c. in whatever direction the wind is blowing.
- [ ] d. away from a fuel source.

_____

**Clarifying Devices**   5   In the last paragraph, the writer again refers to the fire as a living creature by saying that it
- [ ] a. can be blown around by the wind.
- [ ] b. dwarf a man's best efforts.
- [ ] c. heats the air above it.
- [ ] d. may still win the struggle.

_____

**Vocabulary in Context**   6   A <u>turbulent</u> wind
- [ ] a. blows in all directions.
- [ ] b. is extremely hot.
- [ ] c. circles like a tornado.
- [ ] d. has little strength.

_____

**Add your scores for questions 1–6. Enter the total here and on the graph on page 218.**      **Total Score**      _____

**155**

# 78 Garlic: The Magic Cure-All

Once you have smelled the delicious aroma of garlic, you'll never forget it. It is an herb that is widely used in cooking and salads. You may hear of people using it to improve their health. Some say it even has magical powers. These magical powers were known of even in ancient times. For instance, a Roman soldier would not go into battle without first eating some garlic. The Romans believed that garlic gave a person strength and courage. Whether or not the soldiers fought any better because of their garlic eating, however, is unknown. Nevertheless, this Roman habit may have been frightening to the enemies.

The period of the Middle Ages was <u>fraught</u> with superstition. During the frightening Black Plague, people ate bushels of garlic as protection against the dread disease. Garlic was thought of as a cure-all. For example, people who feared vampires, werewolves, and the evil eye of a witch would wear cloves of garlic wrapped in cloth and hung around their necks.

Even today, garlic is used in various old-fashioned, cure-all remedies. A syrup made from garlic is said to cure colds. A clove of garlic wrapped in a wet cloth and kept on the chest will relieve the discomforts of bronchitis. Garlic has even been put to use in agriculture. Garlic scattered in the soil around peach trees is supposed to protect the trees from harmful pests. And garlic really can be soothing when rubbed on insect bites.

In actuality, garlic's value is not all superstition. Garlic does contain an antibiotic—allium—that doctors use to lower high blood pressure in patients.

| Main Idea | 1 | | Answer | Score |
|---|---|---|---|---|
| | | Mark the *main idea* | M | 15 |
| | | Mark the statement that is *too broad* | B | 5 |
| | | Mark the statement that is *too narrow* | N | 5 |

|  |  | Answer | Score |
|---|---|---|---|
| a. | Many superstitions surround the use of garlic. | ☐ | ____ |
| b. | Garlic was a main ingredient in many old-fashioned remedies. | ☐ | ____ |
| c. | Some people believe that certain herbs have magical powers. | ☐ | ____ |

**Score 15 points for each correct answer.**                    **Score**

**Subject Matter**    **2**    This passage discusses the uses of
  ☐ a. allium.
  ☐ b. superstition.
  ☐ c. garlic.
  ☐ d. magic herb.                                          _____

**Supporting**    **3**    The allium contained in garlic is good for
**Details**
  ☐ a. diabetes.
  ☐ b. high blood pressure.
  ☐ c. headaches.
  ☐ d. ulcers.                                              _____

**Conclusion**    **4**    It is evident from this passage that
  ☐ a. garlic has magical powers.
  ☐ b. the Roman soldiers owed their victories to
      garlic.
  ☐ c. garlic has had many uses throughout history.
  ☐ d. garlic is a valuable cure-all medicine.             _____

**Clarifying**    **5**    The writer shows the diverse uses of garlic by
**Devices**
  ☐ a. giving examples.
  ☐ b. tracing its evolution.
  ☐ c. speculating.
  ☐ d. proving its value.                                  _____

**Vocabulary**    **6**    As used in this passage, the word <u>fraught</u> means
**in Context**
  ☐ a. devoid.
  ☐ b. characterized.
  ☐ c. scattered.
  ☐ d. full of.                                            _____

**Add your scores for questions 1–6. Enter the total here**    **Total**
**and on the graph on page 218.**                              **Score**
                                                          _____

# 79 Cover Your Eyes!

Nature has devised many ways to protect creatures' eyes. The most common protection is the eyelid—a fold of skin that closes over the eye, protecting it from damage. Eyelashes are useful for keeping out dust and other irritants, and tears wash away any particles that get through the other defenses.

Some creatures, including most birds, have three eyelids. The upper and lower lids act like human lids and keep out twigs, dirt, and sand. The third eyelid, however, is a semitransparent tissue that crosses over the eye from the inside corner to the outside corner. Because of this protective membrane, birds seldom have to blink. They close their eyes only when they go to sleep. In ducks, this third eyelid serves as an underwater diving mask that helps the ducks find food.

Most fish and snakes have no eyelids at all. Instead, a hard glassy covering protects their eyes. In fish, water constantly sweeps away dirt from the covering. And a snake's eyesight is usually so bad that a little dirt <u>obscuring</u> its vision does not disturb it greatly.

Eyelashes defend the eye by shading it from glare. They also act like miniature brushes to remove dust. Camels have lashes that are four inches long to protect their eyes from windblown sand in the desert.

| Main Idea | 1 | | |
|---|---|---|---|
| | | Answer | Score |
| | **Mark the *main idea*** | M | 15 |
| | **Mark the statement that is *too broad*** | B | 5 |
| | **Mark the statement that is *too narrow*** | N | 5 |
| | a. Creatures' eyes are protected in a number of different ways. | ☐ | _____ |
| | b. Nature has provided many kinds of protection for living creatures. | ☐ | _____ |
| | c. Eyelids are one of the most important forms of eye protection. | ☐ | _____ |

**Subject Matter**    **2**    Another good title for this passage would be
- ☐ a. Look Out!
- ☐ b. Birds' Eyes.
- ☐ c. Eyes in the Night.
- ☐ d. Protecting the Eye.      _____

**Supporting Details**    **3**    A camel has long eyelashes
- ☐ a. to keep windblown sand out of its eyes.
- ☐ b. that get in the way of its sight.
- ☐ c. to help it see better.
- ☐ d. to attract other camels.      _____

**Conclusion**    **4**    The writer implies that eyelids are
- ☐ a. not found on lizards.
- ☐ b. nice to look at.
- ☐ c. always covered with eyelashes.
- ☐ d. the most effective eye protection.      _____

**Clarifying Devices**    **5**    The author compares the duck's third eyelid to a
- ☐ a. tissue.
- ☐ b. glass covering.
- ☐ c. tiny brush.
- ☐ d. diving mask.      _____

**Vocabulary in Context**    **6**    <u>Obscuring</u> in this selection means
- ☐ a. hiding.
- ☐ b. blocking.
- ☐ c. confusing.
- ☐ d. delaying.      _____

**Add your scores for questions 1–6. Enter the total here and on the graph on page 218.**      **Total Score**    _____

# 80 Flying Tigers

Hawks and falcons are the wolves and tigers of the bird kingdom. They are meat-eaters that rely on strength and skill to catch their unwary victims. These birds have unusually good eyesight, great skill in flight, and sharp beaks and talons that quickly end the struggles of their prey.

The hawks—a family that includes the bald eagle—tend to be large birds that hunt by soaring and gliding high in the air until they spot their prey on the ground. Then they drop down in a fast and accurate swoop, giving no warning until their wings flash open to break their fall, and their sharp talons close on their victims.

Falcons are usually smaller than hawks. They have long, narrow wings designed for very fast flight. This family includes the peregrine falcon, called the bird of kings, which has been trained to hunt for the royalty of Europe and Africa for centuries. The peregrine, in its swoop upon its prey, has been <u>clocked</u> at speeds of over 100 miles per hour.

Until recently, hawks and falcons had suffered from people's war on insects. Small animals ate the insects that had been sprayed with chemicals; then these were eaten by larger animals that were in turn eaten by the birds of prey. After the hawks had eaten a number of these animals, the chemicals had a deadly effect. The birds began to lay eggs with very thin shells that broke when the birds tried to hatch them. But now, due to careful efforts to restore the hawk and falcon population, these birds are beginning to make a comeback.

| Main Idea | 1 | Answer | Score |
|---|---|---|---|
| | Mark the *main idea* | M | 15 |
| | Mark the statement that is *too broad* | B | 5 |
| | Mark the statement that is *too narrow* | N | 5 |
| | a. Hawks and falcons are powerful birds. | ☐ | ___ |
| | b. Hawks and falcons survive by their great strength and skill. | ☐ | ___ |
| | c. Hawks and falcons swoop down upon their prey. | ☐ | ___ |

**Subject Matter**    **2**    Another good title for this selection would be
- ☐ a. The Rulers of the Skies.
- ☐ b. Bird Eaters.
- ☐ c. Wolves and Tigers.
- ☐ d. Beware of the Falcon.    _____

**Supporting Details**    **3**    The chemicals that entered the bodies of hawks and falcons through the animals they ate eventually
- ☐ a. wore off and disappeared.
- ☐ b. caused them to lay eggs with very thin shells.
- ☐ c. made them immune to diseases.
- ☐ d. caused them to die.    _____

**Conclusion**    **4**    From the passage, it appears that the writer
- ☐ a. thinks hawks and falcons are cruel.
- ☐ b. wants small animals to stop eating insects.
- ☐ c. thinks that the hawk and falcon population is increasing.
- ☐ d. wants to study the effects of chemicals.    _____

**Clarifying Devices**    **5**    Hawks and falcons are called "flying tigers" because they
- ☐ a. quickly attack and kill their prey.
- ☐ b. often have striped bodies.
- ☐ c. fly faster than tigers run.
- ☐ d. are very protective of their young.    _____

**Vocabulary in Context**    **6**    <u>Clocked</u>, as used in this passage, means
- ☐ a. snapped.
- ☐ b. alarmed.
- ☐ c. timed.
- ☐ d. clicked.    _____

**Add your scores for questions 1–6. Enter the total here and on the graph on page 218.**

Total
Score    _____

# 81 A Bird That Never Really Dies

The phoenix was one of the most magnificent birds that ever lived. Unfortunately for bird watchers, the grand phoenix actually lived only in the imaginations of the ancient Greeks and Egyptians.

According to Greek mythology, only one phoenix at a time lived on earth. The phoenix, a male, was brightly colored, with gold and red feathers. Legend has it that the single bird lived for exactly five hundred years. Just before it was to die, it would build a nest. The mythical bird's last task was to sit patiently on the nest, waiting for the sun to ignite the dry twigs and set the nest ablaze. But as the proud phoenix sacrificed itself in flame, a tiny worm would crawl from beneath the ashes. This worm grew into a new phoenix. Its first task was to gather up its father's ashes and bury them in the temple of the Egyptian sun god in Heliopolis, the City of the Sun. Each reborn phoenix lived out the remainder of its life in Arabia.

Today, the phoenix symbolizes <u>immortality</u>. Someone who succeeds where he or she had previously failed is often referred to as a phoenix.

| Main Idea | 1 | Answer | Score |
|---|---|---|---|
| | **Mark the *main idea*** | **M** | 15 |
| | **Mark the statement that is *too broad*** | **B** | 5 |
| | **Mark the statement that is *too narrow*** | **N** | 5 |

a. Greek myths contain many stories of magical beasts and creatures. ☐ _____

b. The phoenix is a mythological bird that lived for five hundred years and then sacrificed itself to give birth to a new phoenix. ☐ _____

c. A new phoenix was born from the ashes of the old phoenix. ☐ _____

**Score 15 points for each correct answer.**  **Score**

Subject Matter   2   This passage discusses an ancient
    ☐ a. king.
    ☐ b. myth.
    ☐ c. fairy tale.
    ☐ d. god.                                        _____

Supporting   3   Most of a phoenix's life was supposedly spent in
Details
    ☐ a. Greece.
    ☐ b. Egypt.
    ☐ c. Heliopolis.
    ☐ d. Arabia.                                     _____

Conclusion   4   Someone who is called a phoenix today
    ☐ a. has come back from a defeat.
    ☐ b. is probably immortal.
    ☐ c. thinks he or she can live forever.
    ☐ d. is not well liked by colleagues.             _____

Clarifying   5   The life of the phoenix is described
Devices
    ☐ a. with the use of facts.
    ☐ b. in a humorous way.
    ☐ c. in an unclear way.
    ☐ d. step-by-step.                               _____

Vocabulary   6   A person possessing <u>immortality</u> could live
in Context
    ☐ a. for eight hundred years.
    ☐ b. forever.
    ☐ c. for two hundred years.
    ☐ d. almost as long as the phoenix.              _____

**Add your scores for questions 1–6. Enter the total here**   **Total**
**and on the graph on page 219.**   **Score**   _____

# 82 The Beginnings of Television

Are your parents old enough to remember watching "Howdy Doody Time"? Can your grandparents recall dramas they saw on "Studio One"? These are some of the better-known shows from the very earliest days of television.

The capacity to send and receive moving pictures via airwaves was developed years earlier, but television only began showing up in people's homes in about 1947. (World War II, which had halted their production, ended in 1945.) These very early TVs had screens that were only a few inches wide, but people snapped them up as fast as they could be made.

What kinds of shows were available? "Howdy Doody" was a children's show with puppets, live characters, and a host named Buffalo Bob. "Studio One" featured full-length dramas in which such stars as James Dean and Warren Beatty made early appearances. Both of these shows debuted in the 1940s. So did an early version of the news show "Meet the Press."

Most pioneering television programs were live. This meant if actors forgot their lines or a prop got knocked over, the audience got to see it anyway. Since some of the most popular early shows were comedies, the mistakes could make the programs even funnier. Did Milton Berle in "The Texaco Star Theater" really mean to fall off that piano bench? Was Imogene Coca's hat in a "Your Show of Shows" skit really supposed to catch in a closing door? Since the stars laughed right along with the audience, you could never be sure.

| Main Idea | 1 | | Answer | Score |
|---|---|---|---|---|
| | Mark the *main idea* | | M | 15 |
| | Mark the statement that is *too broad* | | B | 5 |
| | Mark the statement that is *too narrow* | | N | 5 |

a. Most early TV programs were shown live. ☐ _____

b. Televisions became widespread after World War II. ☐ _____

c. Early TV programs were a mix of children's shows, comedy, dramas, and news. ☐ _____

**Subject Matter**   **2**   This passage focuses on

☐ a. some of the earliest television shows.

☐ b. a history of the development of television.

☐ c. why television became popular.

☐ d. differences between TV and radio programs.   _____

**Supporting Details**   **3**   Shows like "Studio One" and "Meet the Press" started on television in

☐ a. the early 1940s.

☐ b. the late 1940s.

☐ c. the early 1950s.

☐ d. the late 1950s.   _____

**Conclusion**   **4**   This passage suggests that early comedy shows

☐ a. used slapstick and silly visual jokes.

☐ b. were not terribly funny.

☐ c. usually involved two characters talking to each other.

☐ d. were not on the air for too many years.   _____

**Clarifying Devices**   **5**   The writer tries to capture your interest in the first paragraph by

☐ a. mentioning several stars.

☐ b. describing a dramatic incident.

☐ c. comparing and contrasting two programs.

☐ d. asking specific questions.   _____

**Vocabulary in Context**   **6**   Debuted means

☐ a. first publicly appeared.

☐ b. ended.

☐ c. became popular.

☐ d. entertained.   _____

**Add your scores for questions 1–6. Enter the total here and on the graph on page 219.**     **Total Score**   _____

# 83 A Reward for Heroism

When soldiers distinguish themselves for bravery in a combat situation, they may be awarded the Medal of Honor. Bestowed by the President and Congress, the Medal of Honor is the highest military award the country can give. Only about 3,400 soldiers have received it.

The Medal of Honor was first presented by President Abraham Lincoln during the Civil War. At that time it was given to a whole regiment of soldiers—over eight hundred in all. The purpose was not really to honor the soldiers, however; it was more a way to keep them on duty! In 1916, Congress changed the function of the medal to be a reward for heroism. The earlier medals were taken back. Since then medals have been awarded in every war except the Persian Gulf War. The most recent recipients were two army sergeants who fought and were killed in Somalia. They received their medals <u>posthumously</u>.

Here are some of the deeds for which the medal has been awarded. A soldier in World War II killed eleven Germans and captured over thirty others—all in a single battle. One who was captured during the Vietnam War wounded and almost killed himself rather than betray information about his troops. A soldier in Korea led a charge up an enemy hill while being shot at. Some soldiers have thrown themselves on hand grenades in order to protect their fellow soldiers. Others have performed daring feats of rescue.

Once a year, the living medal winners meet at a formal reunion. They feel that the medal binds them together like members of a (very heroic) family.

| Main Idea | 1 | | Answer | Score |
|---|---|---|---|---|
| | | **Mark the *main idea*** | M | 15 |
| | | **Mark the statement that is *too broad*** | B | 5 |
| | | **Mark the statement that is *too narrow*** | N | 5 |

a. Many soldiers are deserving of awards for bravery. ☐ _____

b. The Medal of Honor has been awarded to brave American soldiers through many wars. ☐ _____

c. Many medal recipients have rescued their fellow soldiers in battle. ☐ _____

**Score 15 points for each correct answer.**  **Score**

**Subject Matter**  **2**  This passage is basically a(n)
- [ ] a. argument in favor of awarding the Medal of Honor.
- [ ] b. history of the Medal of Honor.
- [ ] c. history of American wars.
- [ ] d. story about Abraham Lincoln.  _____

**Supporting Details**  **3**  The Medal of Honor was originally awarded during
- [ ] a. the Civil War.
- [ ] b. the Persian Gulf War.
- [ ] c. World War I.
- [ ] d. World War II.  _____

**Conclusion**  **4**  The first soldiers to receive the Medal of Honor were
- [ ] a. enthusiastic soldiers.
- [ ] b. not very enthusaistic soldiers.
- [ ] c. very young.
- [ ] d. very old.  _____

**Clarifying Devices**  **5**  The writer explains how the medal may be won by
- [ ] a. giving several examples.
- [ ] b. telling the story of one soldier.
- [ ] c. telling about its first recipients.
- [ ] d. mentioning Abraham Lincoln.  _____

**Vocabulary in Context**  **6**  <u>Posthumously</u> means
- [ ] a. at the start of battle.
- [ ] b. after death.
- [ ] c. in a special ceremony in front of Congress.
- [ ] d. with their comrades.  _____

**Add your scores for questions 1–6. Enter the total here and on the graph on page 219.**  **Total Score**  _____

# 84 I Wouldn't Try It Again

He shouldn't have come back alive. Captain J. H. Hedley was a British pilot in World War I. He fell victim to a bit of misfortune that would have been enough to kill anyone. Yet with bad luck staring him in the face, good luck was coming up fast on his tail.

Captain Hedley was flying a mission over Germany with his copilot, a Canadian flyer named Makepeace. Suddenly they were surrounded by a group of German fighters. Makepeace, an experienced pilot, knew he had to take the plane into a dive straight down in order to slip away from the Germans. <u>Inexplicably</u>, Hedley was caught unaware by his copilot's maneuver. He was thrown sharply out of his seat and out of the plane. Makepeace sadly counted Hedley a dead man and continued trying to avoid the enemy.

Suddenly, Makepeace spotted Hedley clinging to the tail of the plane. Hedley hung on and pulled himself back into the plane when it leveled off. Makepeace was stunned by the sight of Hedley, but he kept his composure enough to get them out of trouble and out of Germany. The best explanation for Hedley's reprieve was that the plane's sudden vertical dive had created a vacuum in the air behind it. Hedley fell into the vacuum and was pulled along until he grabbed the tail and made his fantastic reentry.

| Main Idea | 1 | | Answer | Score |
|---|---|---|---|---|
| | Mark the *main idea* | | M | 15 |
| | Mark the statement that is *too broad* | | B | 5 |
| | Mark the statement that is *too narrow* | | N | 5 |

a. Captain Hedley was thrown from an open cockpit plane. ☐ _____

b. People sometimes survive terribly dangerous accidents. ☐ _____

c. Captain Hedley was thrown out of an airplane and was able to get back inside unharmed. ☐ _____

**Subject Matter**   2   This passage is about
☐ a. World War II.
☐ b. the adventures of Makepeace and Hedley.
☐ c. the miraculous fall and recovery of Captain Hedley.
☐ d. World War I.                                       _____

**Supporting Details**   3   In World War I, Britain and Canada were
☐ a. afraid of each other.
☐ b. in competition.
☐ c. on the same side.
☐ d. fighting each other.                               _____

**Conclusion**   4   We can conclude that Hedley's escape from death was mostly due to
☐ a. faith.
☐ b. luck.
☐ c. science.
☐ d. Makepeace's flying ability.                        _____

**Clarifying Devices**   5   The writer begins the passage by
☐ a. making a series of interesting statements without explaining them.
☐ b. telling a joke.
☐ c. asking some questions.
☐ d. quoting a war veteran.                             _____

**Vocabulary in Context**   6   Something that happens <u>inexplicably</u> happens in a manner that is
☐ a. ridiculous.
☐ b. memorable.
☐ c. unforgivable.
☐ d. unexplainable.                                     _____

**Add your scores for questions 1–6. Enter the total here and on the graph on page 219.**     Total Score     _____

# 85 Eye Facts

There are many commonly held beliefs about eyeglasses and eyesight that are not proven facts. For instance, some people believe that wearing glasses too soon weakens the eyes. But there is no evidence to show that the structure of eyes is changed by wearing glasses at a young age. Wearing the wrong glasses, however, can prove harmful. Studies show that for adults there is no danger, but children can <u>develop</u> loss of vision if they have glasses inappropriate for their eyes.

We have all heard some of the common myths about how eyesight gets bad. Most people believe that reading in dim light causes poor eyesight, but that is untrue. Too little light makes the eyes work harder, so they do get tired and strained. Eyestrain also results from reading a lot, reading in bed, and watching too much television. However, although eyestrain may cause some pain or headaches, it does not permanently damage eyesight.

Another myth about eyes is that they can be replaced, or transferred from one person to another. There are close to one million nerve fibers that connect the eyeball to the brain; as of yet, it is impossible to attach them all in a new person. Only certain parts of the eye—the cornea and the retina—can be replaced. But if we keep clearing up the myths and learning more about the eyes, someday a full transplant may be possible!

| Main Idea | 1 | Answer | Score |
|---|---|---|---|
| | **Mark the *main idea*** | M | 15 |
| | **Mark the statement that is *too broad*** | B | 5 |
| | **Mark the statement that is *too narrow*** | N | 5 |

a. People have many false notions about the eyes and sight.   ☐   _____

b. There are many things about the body that are not completely understood.   ☐   _____

c. There are several causes of eyestrain.   ☐   _____

**Score 15 points for each correct answer.**          **Score**

**Subject Matter**          **2**          This passage is mostly about
- ☐ a. different types of eyeglasses.
- ☐ b. a visit to the eye doctor.
- ☐ c. myths about eyesight.
- ☐ d. cornea transplants.          _____

**Supporting Details**          **3**          One cause of eyestrain mentioned in the passage is
- ☐ a. wearing contact lenses too long.
- ☐ b. going to the movies.
- ☐ c. reading a lot.
- ☐ d. not visiting your eye doctor.          _____

**Conclusion**          **4**          From this passage one can conclude that
- ☐ a. doctors are still learning things about eyesight.
- ☐ b. headaches are only caused by eyestrain.
- ☐ c. everyone should wear glasses.
- ☐ d. people only believe things that are proven facts.          _____

**Clarifying Devices**          **5**          "Commonly held beliefs" are
- ☐ a. ideas that only low class people believe.
- ☐ b. ideas that most people believe.
- ☐ c. beliefs that have something in common.
- ☐ d. foolish beliefs.          _____

**Vocabulary in Context**          **6**          The word <u>develop</u> is used to mean
- ☐ a. become larger.
- ☐ b. create.
- ☐ c. train.
- ☐ d. acquire.          _____

**Add your scores for questions 1–6. Enter the total here and on the graph on page 219.**          **Total Score**          _____

# 86 Life on Other Planets?

Since early times, people have been fascinated with the idea of life existing somewhere else besides Earth. Until recently, scientists believed that <u>extraterrestrial</u> life was just a hopeful dream. But now they are beginning to locate places where life could form. In 1997, they saw evidence of planets near other stars like the sun. Planets are places that might have the basic conditions for life. But scientists now think that life could be even nearer, in our own solar system.

One place scientists are studying very closely is Europa, a moon of Jupiter. Space probes have provided evidence that Europa has a large ocean under its surface. The probes have also made scientists think that under its surface Europa has a rocky core giving off volcanic heat. Water and heat from volcanic activity are two basic conditions needed for life to form. A third is certain basic chemicals such as carbon, oxygen, and nitrogen. Comets and meteorites carrying these chemicals have certainly hit Europa at some point. So scientists think chemicals might be lying at the bottom of Europa's ocean. They may have already created life—or may be about to.

You may wonder if light is also needed for life to form. Until recently, scientists thought that light was essential. But now places have been found on Earth that are in total blackness, such as caves several miles beneath the surface. And bacteria, primitive forms of life, have been seen there. So the lack of light in Europa's subsurface ocean doesn't automatically rule out life forming.

Needless to say, scientists want to learn more about Europa. They are continuing to study it closely.

| Main Idea | 1 | | | |
|---|---|---|---|---|
| | | | Answer | Score |
| | Mark the *main idea* | | M | 15 |
| | Mark the statement that is *too broad* | | B | 5 |
| | Mark the statement that is *too narrow* | | N | 5 |

a. Europa seems to have the conditions necessary to support life. ☐ _____

b. There should be life somewhere else in the universe besides Earth. ☐ _____

c. Europa has probably been hit by comets or meteorites. ☐ _____

**Subject Matter**   **2**   This passage is mainly about
- ☐ a. life on other planets.
- ☐ b. space probes exploring our solar system.
- ☐ c. whether light is needed for life to develop.
- ☐ d. life forming on Europa.

_____

**Supporting Details**   **3**   Two conditions necessary for life are
- ☐ a. light and water.
- ☐ b. water and heat.
- ☐ c. light and chemicals like nitrogen.
- ☐ d. heat and bacteria.

_____

**Conclusion**   **4**   If scientists have their way, there will be
- ☐ a. more space probes to Europa.
- ☐ b. settlements on planets like Mars.
- ☐ c. more publicity about recent space discoveries.
- ☐ d. better control over the budget for space exploration.

_____

**Clarifying Devices**   **5**   In the second paragraph, the phrase "a rocky core" means
- ☐ a. a structure that almost resembles an apple.
- ☐ b. the innermost part.
- ☐ c. stones covering Europa's surface.
- ☐ d. a mountain on the surface that is about to explode.

_____

**Vocabulary in Context**   **6**   The word <u>extraterrestrial</u> means
- ☐ a. beyond the Earth.
- ☐ b. on the Earth.
- ☐ c. inside the Earth.
- ☐ d. on a UFO.

_____

**Add your scores for questions 1–6. Enter the total here and on the graph on page 219.**   **Total Score**

_____

# 87 Early Passenger Planes

The Wright brothers made their first flight in 1903. But they probably had little idea that one day planes would transport people all over the world.

In the early days of aviation, dirigibles—huge gas-filled balloons—were used to transport most passengers. The first recorded passenger service by airplane came in 1914, when for $5 a passenger could fly across Tampa Bay in a two-seater plane. A somewhat larger passenger plane was built around the same time in Russia. This plane had an open deck along its back—a place where passengers could walk, if they dared, during the flight. Since nearly all early flights took place in cold, drafty planes, passengers were often supplied with leather helmets, gloves, and even hot-water bottles.

Early passenger flights had two serious <u>limitations</u>. To be safe, they could not fly very high, and they could not fly at night. So flying across the United States required a series of short hops from one destination to the next. As airplane construction improved, so did passenger choices. The Boeing 247, an all-metal plane introduced in 1933, carried ten passengers and could go almost 200 miles per hour. Shortly afterward came the Douglas DC-3. This plane was an updated version of one that had sleeper berths for overnight travel. It could hold twenty-one passengers and fly above 5,000 feet. DC-3s were the first planes large enough to operate at a profit.

When jet airliners were introduced in the 1950s, flights became longer, faster, and cheaper. Air travel was now a possibility for just about everyone.

**Main Idea**    1

| | Answer | Score |
|---|---|---|
| **Mark the *main idea*** | M | 15 |
| **Mark the statement that is *too broad*** | B | 5 |
| **Mark the statement that is *too narrow*** | N | 5 |

a. Early passenger planes could not fly high, nor could they fly at night. ☐ _____

b. The history of flight involves many types of planes. ☐ _____

c. Passenger planes developed steadily through the first half of the century. ☐ _____

**Subject Matter**   **2**   This passage is mostly about
- ☐ a. how people learned to fly.
- ☐ b. different kinds of early passenger planes.
- ☐ c. safety features of early planes.
- ☐ d. magic herbs.

_____

**Supporting Details**   **3**   The first flights made just for passengers occurred in
- ☐ a. 1914.
- ☐ b. 1903.
- ☐ c. 1950.
- ☐ d. 1933.

_____

**Conclusion**   **4**   Sleeper berths in airplanes
- ☐ a. were popular from the very beginning.
- ☐ b. did not last too long.
- ☐ c. were only for the very rich.
- ☐ d. were practical, but expensive to build.

_____

**Clarifying Devices**   **5**   As used in this passage, the expression "a series of short hops" refers to
- ☐ a. airplanes.
- ☐ b. pilots.
- ☐ c. flights.
- ☐ d. schedules.

_____

**Vocabulary in Context**   **6**   A good synonym for <u>limitations</u> in this passage would be
- ☐ a. controls.
- ☐ b. shortcomings.
- ☐ c. characteristics.
- ☐ d. descriptions.

_____

**Add your scores for questions 1–6. Enter the total here and on the graph on page 219.**      **Total Score**

_____

# 88 The Giant Saguaro

The giant saguaro may well symbolize the desert, but it is more than a symbol, even more than a plant. To a host of creatures—birds, mammals, and insects—the stately saguaro is home. It is an apartment house—and an air-conditioned one at that.

A pair of Gila woodpeckers once constructed an apartment atop a twenty-five-foot saguaro. These carvers cut a hole two inches in diameter into the cactus. They bored straight for about three inches, then turned sharply downward and dug a chamber about nine inches deep and four inches wide.

White pulp exuding sticky sap lined the hole. Over the next few months, the sap hardened to form a dry, tough callous all around the hole, making the hard walls and a floor for the apartment. In April, the birds came back to move into their apartment and get started on the important business of raising babies. On the hard, bare floor of the hole, the female laid four white eggs and sat on them in cool comfort.

Within the plant, behind the tough lining, the living sap of the cactus flowed. This liquid kept the temperature inside the hole well below the hot midday temperature outside. All day the cactus absorbed heat from the sun, but the interior of the hole remained cooler than the <u>sweltering</u> outdoors. At night, when the outside heat quickly escaped into the sky, the woodpeckers were snug in their house, heated now by the warmed cactus sap.

| Main Idea | 1 | | |
|---|---|---|---|
| | | **Answer** | **Score** |
| | Mark the *main idea* | M | 15 |
| | Mark the statement that is *too broad* | B | 5 |
| | Mark the statement that is *too narrow* | N | 5 |

a. A small chamber inside a saguaro will remain cool even in the desert heat. ☐ _____

b. The saguaro is a very useful plant. ☐ _____

c. A saguaro can become an air-conditioned apartment for birds and other animals. ☐ _____

**Subject Matter**  **2**  Another good title for this selection would be
☐ a. Woodpecker's Endurance.
☐ b. This Apartment Is for the Birds.
☐ c. Symbols of the Desert.
☐ d. Want to Buy a Cactus?                        _____

**Supporting Details**  **3**  The hardened sap becomes the
☐ a. food for the young.
☐ b. air conditioning for the apartment.
☐ c. door of the apartment.
☐ d. walls and floor of the apartment.           _____

**Conclusion**  **4**  The author seems to admire the
☐ a. ideal suitability of the woodpecker's home.
☐ b. giant saguaro.
☐ c. desert's cruelty.
☐ d. intelligence of woodpeckers.                 _____

**Clarifying Devices**  **5**  The author develops this passage
☐ a. by showing contrasts.
☐ b. by using negative arguments.
☐ c. by describing an incident.
☐ d. by making a comparison.                      _____

**Vocabulary in Context**  **6**  Sweltering means
☐ a. very dry.
☐ b. extremely hot.
☐ c. cruel.
☐ d. cold and icy.                                _____

**Add your scores for questions 1–6. Enter the total here and on the graph on page 219.**  **Total Score**  _____

# 89 Horse Sense

The crowd stirred and whispered in awe as, on the stage, the horse slowly tapped out the beat. Everyone become tense and quiet as the number of taps neared the correct answer to the horse trainer's question. After the final tap, the horse paused, seemed to look around, and stopped. The crowd went wild!

The horse's name was Clever Hans, the Educated Horse, and he was featured in a vaudeville act in the early 1900s in Europe. When asked a complicated mathematical question by his owner, Clever Hans would tap out the correct answer with his hooves. For example, if the answer was sixty-eight, Hans would tap out six with his left hoof and eight with his right hoof. Even more remarkable, the owner would leave the room after asking the question, so there could be no secret signal between owner and horse. A mere animal seemed to be accomplishing a highly technical human skill!

It wasn't until years later that the secret of the trick was revealed. The owner had trained Clever Hans to respond to slight signals. The horse became so sensitive that he learned when to stop from the crowd's reaction. Members of the audience would unknowingly <u>start</u> or give some other unconscious signal when Hans reached the right answer. Modern scientists now warn against the Clever Hans syndrome, whereby researchers unwittingly give clues to their animal subjects about actions they would like to see performed!

**Main Idea**     1

|  | Answer | Score |
|---|---|---|
| Mark the *main idea* | M | 15 |
| Mark the statement that is *too broad* | B | 5 |
| Mark the statement that is *too narrow* | N | 5 |

a. Clever Hans used audience clues to perform seemingly impossible counting tricks.   ☐   _____

b. Animals can be trained to do many tricks.   ☐   _____

c. Clever Hans used his hoofs to tap out the correct answer.   ☐   _____

**Subject Matter** 2 This passage is mainly about
☐ a. animal intelligence.
☐ b. mathematical skills.
☐ c. Clever Hans.
☐ d. ways to trick audiences. _____

**Supporting Details** 3 The Clever Hans syndrome is a danger to be avoided by
☐ a. audiences.
☐ b. researchers.
☐ c. veterinarians.
☐ d. mathematicians. _____

**Conclusion** 4 Clever Hans's real talent was
☐ a. his sensitivity to crowd reactions.
☐ b. adding large sums.
☐ c. standing quietly on stage.
☐ d. obeying his owner. _____

**Clarifying Devices** 5 The first paragraph of this passage is
☐ a. a first-person account.
☐ b. a dramatic account.
☐ c. an understatement.
☐ d. a scientific finding. _____

**Vocabulary in Context** 6 As used in this passage, the word start means
☐ a. cry out.
☐ b. begin.
☐ c. applaud.
☐ d. jerk. _____

**Add your scores for questions 1–6. Enter the total here and on the graph on page 219.** **Total Score** _____

# 90 Our Inner Senses

If we had to rely on only five senses for survival, we would be in very sad shape indeed. We wouldn't know up from down. We wouldn't know when to eat or drink. We wouldn't know what our muscles were doing or what position our limbs were in. We wouldn't know when our body was damaged, because we wouldn't feel pain. We might freeze to death without even a shiver or overheat without a drop of sweat. The five senses—touch, taste, smell, hearing, and sight—respond only to stimulation from the outside world, but the inside world of our bodies must also receive and respond to important messages.

Our internal senses keep us alive and enable us to use our external senses. In effect, the internal senses tell our brains how to run our bodies. Hunger and thirst register in a part of the brain called the hypothalamus when a lack of food chemicals is detected in the blood.

Another internal sense that controls our balance is maintained by three fluid-filled loops in the inner ear. Changes in position and gravity affect the motion of this liquid and trigger changes in the brain. A sense called kinesthesia lets us know the relative positions of parts of our bodies. Even our breathing is triggered by a sense that identifies an overabundance of carbon dioxide and a lack of oxygen in the blood.

No one has been able to count the number of internal senses. The presence of delicate internal senses shows just how marvelously complex we human beings are.

| Main Idea | 1 | Answer | Score |
|---|---|---|---|
| | Mark the *main idea* | M | 15 |
| | Mark the statement that is *too broad* | B | 5 |
| | Mark the statement that is *too narrow* | N | 5 |

a. Many things are needed to make our bodies work right.  ☐ _____

b. Our bodies are controlled by internal senses as well as by the five external senses.  ☐ _____

c. The internal senses control balance and breathing.  ☐ _____

**Score 15 points for each correct answer.**          **Score**

**Subject Matter**  **2**  This passage deals mostly with the
- [ ] a. internal senses.
- [ ] b. sense of balance.
- [ ] c. five senses.
- [ ] d. brain's function.                          _____

**Supporting Details**  **3**  Hunger is caused by
- [ ] a. too much food and water in the body.
- [ ] b. a lack of oxygen in the blood.
- [ ] c. seeing or thinking about food.
- [ ] d. a lack of certain chemicals in the blood.   _____

**Conclusion**  **4**  The passage implies that there are many senses we
- [ ] a. can use only in emergencies.
- [ ] b. may not understand at present.
- [ ] c. never realize we have.
- [ ] d. do not actively use in everyday living.     _____

**Clarifying Devices**  **5**  In the second paragraph, the term "in effect" means
- [ ] a. in fact.
- [ ] b. it is doubtful.
- [ ] c. without reason.
- [ ] d. often.                                      _____

**Vocabulary in Context**  **6**  <u>Register</u> in this passage most nearly means
- [ ] a. ignite.
- [ ] b. activate.
- [ ] c. signal.
- [ ] d. revise.                                     _____

**Add your scores for questions 1–6. Enter the total here**   **Total**
**and on the graph on page 219.**                              **Score**        _____

# 91 Countries in Miniature

Did you know that, besides larger places like France and Germany, Europe is home to several extremely tiny countries? One contains less than a square mile of land. Another is surrounded on all sides by Italy. Yet each is an independent land, with its own government, trade, and customs.

One of the best known of these little countries is Monaco. It is situated on the Mediterranean Sea and surrounded by France on three sides. Monaco became familiar to Americans when its ruler, Prince Rainier, married the actress Grace Kelly. Rainier's family has ruled Monaco almost continuously since 1297. The land has been independent for over three hundred years. Tourists <u>flock</u> to this tiny country of .75 square miles to enjoy its beautiful harbor and to gamble in its casino.

Andorra, at almost 200 square miles, is considerably larger than Monaco. This country is located in the Pyrenees Mountains, with France on one side and Spain on the other. Potatoes and tobacco are grown in Andorra's steep mountain valleys. One of the products it exports is clothing. Andorra is also known for its excellent skiing locations.

Within the Alps in Central Europe is Liechtenstein, a tiny country of about 30,000 people who speak mostly German. Liechtenstein uses the same money as its neighbor Switzerland, but it has been an independent country since the 1860s. Taxes are low, so many businesses have their headquarters here. The country makes and exports much machinery.

Other small, independent states in Europe are San Marino, Vatican City, and Luxembourg. Each of these has unique qualities as well.

| Main Idea | 1 | | |
|---|---|---|---|
| | | **Answer** | **Score** |
| **Mark the *main idea*** | | M | 15 |
| **Mark the statement that is *too broad*** | | B | 5 |
| **Mark the statement that is *too narrow*** | | N | 5 |

| | | |
|---|---|---|
| a. Europe has several tiny countries. | ☐ | _____ |
| b. The tiny countries in Europe have distinct characteristics and customs. | ☐ | _____ |
| c. A small country may be surrounded on all sides by a larger country. | ☐ | _____ |

**Score 15 points for each correct answer.**           **Score**

**Subject Matter**   **2**   This passage is mostly about
☐ a. how small countries came to be.
☐ b. three small countries in Europe.
☐ c. special products that only small countries produce.
☐ d. small countries situated within mountain ranges.

_____

**Supporting Details**   **3**   Andorra is known for
☐ a. skiing.
☐ b. gambling.
☐ c. low taxes.
☐ d. business headquarters.

_____

**Conclusion**   **4**   This passage leads the reader to believe that one of Grace Kelly's children will probably
☐ a. get into trouble with the law.
☐ b. move to the United States.
☐ c. give up the throne.
☐ d. become ruler of Monaco.

_____

**Clarifying Devices**   **5**   The writer shows that these small countries are all different by
☐ a. giving facts about them.
☐ b. telling about their governments.
☐ c. explaining the characteristics of their citizens.
☐ d. comparing them to San Marino and Vatican City.

_____

**Vocabulary in Context**   **6**   In this passage <u>flock</u> means
☐ a. stampede.
☐ b. move like sheep.
☐ c. go in large numbers.
☐ d. travel.

_____

**Add your scores for questions 1–6. Enter the total here and on the graph on page 219.**     **Total Score**

_____

# 92 Take a Ride on the Interstate

The United States has one of the best highway systems in the world. Interstates connect just about every large and mid-sized city in the country. Did you ever wonder why such a complete system of excellent roads exists?

For an answer, you would have to go back to the early 1920s. In those years just after World War I, military men wanted to build an American highway system for national defense. Such a system could, if necessary, move troops quickly from one area to another. It could also get people out of cities in danger of being bombed. So-called roads of national importance were designated, but they were mostly small country roads. In 1944, Congress passed a bill to upgrade the system but did not fund the plan right away.

In the 1950s, the plan began to become a reality. Over $25 billion was <u>allocated</u>, and construction began on about 40,000 miles of new roads. The idea was to connect the new system to existing expressways and turnpikes, such as the Merritt Parkway in Connecticut and the Pennsylvania Turnpike. And though the system was built mostly to make car travel easier, defense was not forgotten. For instance, highway overpasses had to be high enough to allow trailers carrying military missiles to pass under them.

By 1974, the system was mostly completed. (A few additional roads would come later.) Quick and easy travel between all parts of the country was now possible.

| Main Idea | 1 | Answer | Score |
|---|---|---|---|
| | Mark the *main idea* | M | 15 |
| | Mark the statement that is *too broad* | B | 5 |
| | Mark the statement that is *too narrow* | N | 5 |

a. The excellent interstate system in the United States took many years to plan and build. ☐ _____

b. Good highways are a necessity for efficient transportation. ☐ _____

c. The interstate highway system took over $25 billion to build. ☐ _____

**Score 15 points for each correct answer.**          **Score**

**Subject Matter**   **2**   The passage is mainly about
    ☐ a. the costs of the interstate system.
    ☐ b. early turnpikes and parkways.
    ☐ c. how the interstate system came to be built.
    ☐ d. why Congress was slow in providing money
       for the system.                          _____

**Supporting**   **3**   The original reason for building a highway system
**Details**   was for
    ☐ a. truck transportation.
    ☐ b. car transportation.
    ☐ c. defense.
    ☐ d. showing how Americans could cooperate to
       complete a project.                      _____

**Conclusion**   **4**   The use of the phrase "So-called roads of national
importance" suggests that the writer
    ☐ a. doesn't think those roads were very good.
    ☐ b. believes two-lane highways worked well
       enough at the time.
    ☐ c. does not support the building of the
       interstate system.
    ☐ d. continues to worry about defense.       _____

**Clarifying**   **5**   The information in this passage is presented
**Devices**
    ☐ a. in spatial order.
    ☐ b. in chronological order.
    ☐ c. in cause and effect order.
    ☐ d. from a late date to an earlier date.     _____

**Vocabulary**   **6**   <u>Allocated</u> as used in the passage means
**in Context**
    ☐ a. collected from Congress.
    ☐ b. set aside for a special purpose.
    ☐ c. removed.
    ☐ d. brought up for a vote.                   _____

**Add your scores for questions 1–6. Enter the total here**   **Total**
**and on the graph on page 219.**   **Score**
                                                             _____

# 93 A Fabled African Land

Sometimes people use the expression "going to Timbuktu" when they are traveling to a faraway, isolated place. Did you know that there really is a place called Timbuktu? Not only does it exist, but for centuries it was a very important city in Africa.

Timbuktu is located in the country of Mali, on the southern edge of the Sahara Desert. It was established in around 1100 A.D. as a camp for nomads traveling across the desert. Within two hundred years, it had grown into a fairly large city. Scholarly and religious leaders of Islam, the religion founded by Mohammed, made Timbuktu their home. An important university was built there. There was also a palace for the ruler and many <u>mosques</u> where people could worship. Even when a nonreligious ruler took over, Islamic scholars were used as counselors in religious and legal matters. From Timbuktu, Islam spread across the entire African continent.

Located near the desert and the Niger River, Timbuktu was also a crossroads for trade. In its markets people traded gold, salt, horses, and cloth from all over Africa. The city was a center of learning, wealth, and culture. A visitor in about 1510 described Timbuktu. He observed large buildings, a canal system carrying in fresh water, and the use of pure gold nuggets for money.

After about 1600, Timbuktu began to decline. It was conquered again and again. Today it is a small, rather poor city with few visitors. But still standing are the remains of three huge mosques, symbols of its glorious past.

| Main Idea | 1 | Answer | Score |
|---|---|---|---|
| | Mark the *main idea* | M | 15 |
| | Mark the statement that is *too broad* | B | 5 |
| | Mark the statement that is *too narrow* | N | 5 |

a. Some places that sound unreal actually exist. ☐ _____

b. Timbuktu had many large buildings. ☐ _____

c. Timbuktu was an important religious and trading center. ☐ _____

**Score 15 points for each correct answer.**                    **Score**

**Subject Matter**   **2**   This passage is mainly
    ☐ a. an explanation of why Timbuktu is no
          longer important.
    ☐ b. a history of Timbuktu.
    ☐ c. a summary of trade in the African desert.
    ☐ d. a story told by a traveler to Timbuktu.      _____

**Supporting**   **3**   Timbuktu became an important center of
**Details**
    ☐ a. Judaism.
    ☐ b. Christianity.
    ☐ c. Islam.
    ☐ d. Buddhism.      _____

**Conclusion**   **4**   This passage leads the reader to believe that life in
Timbuktu
    ☐ a. was hard.
    ☐ b. was pleasant.
    ☐ c. involved a lot of warfare.
    ☐ d. required a lot of travel.      _____

**Clarifying**   **5**   In the third paragraph, telling where Timbuktu
**Devices**      was located helps to explain its
    ☐ a. religious importance.
    ☐ b. importance as a trading center.
    ☐ c. climate.
    ☐ d. decline.      _____

**Vocabulary**   **6**   <u>Mosques</u> are
**in Context**
    ☐ a. tents.
    ☐ b. palaces.
    ☐ c. houses of prayer.
    ☐ d. open fields.      _____

**Add your scores for questions 1–6. Enter the total here**   **Total**
**and on the graph on page 219.**   **Score**   _____

# 94 The Great Wild West Show

Gold prospector, Pony Express rider, Civil War army scout: William F. (Buffalo Bill) Cody was a true adventurer of the Wild West. What makes him unusual, however, is that he created a famous show about the West. This show, accurate or not, would be the basis of what many people thought that life in the West was like.

Cody was born in Iowa in 1847. He got his nickname by hunting buffalo to feed the crews building the Kansas Pacific Railroad. One story claims he earned the name by beating out another Buffalo Bill in an eight-hour gun battle. True or not, the story shows the kind of life Cody lived.

In addition to fighting, trapping, and scouting, Cody also acted in stage plays about his exploits. His stage experience led him to create his own show. In 1883, Buffalo Bill's Wild West appeared for the first time. This enormous outdoor production brought to life many dramatic elements of frontier life. Included were a Pony Express ride as well as an exhibition buffalo hunt featuring real buffalo. There was even a re-creation of Custer's Last Stand, with parts played by some of the Native Americans who had actually defeated Custer. The Lakota chief Sitting Bull, who had led the attack on Custer, was part of the show for one year. The sharpshooter Annie Oakley also played a starring role, thrilling audiences with her amazing shooting demonstrations.

Buffalo Bill's show was remarkably successful. He toured the United States and Europe with it for thirty years. Not everyone remembered the West the way he did, but his version influences books, TV shows, and movies even today.

**Main Idea** 1

|  | Answer | Score |
|---|---|---|
| Mark the *main idea* | M | 15 |
| Mark the statement that is *too broad* | B | 5 |
| Mark the statement that is *too narrow* | N | 5 |

a. Buffalo Bill's adventurous life led him to create his successful Wild West show. ☐ _____

b. Some say Buffalo Bill won his name in a gun battle. ☐ _____

c. The Wild West wasn't exactly like most TV westerns show it. ☐ _____

**Score 15 points for each correct answer.**               Score

**Subject Matter**   **2**   The passage is mainly about

☐ a. Buffalo Bill's life and show.

☐ b. building the Kansas Pacific Railroad.

☐ c. the acts that made up the Wild West show.

☐ d. Buffalo Bill's career as a stage actor.                    _____

**Supporting Details**   **3**   A Native American who performed in Buffalo Bill's show was

☐ a. Crazy Horse.

☐ b. Sitting Bull.

☐ c. Chief Joseph.

☐ d. Annie Oakley.                    _____

**Conclusion**   **4**   The writer seems to question whether

☐ a. Native Americans should have participated in Buffalo Bill's show.

☐ b. Buffalo Bill's portrayal of the West was accurate.

☐ c. Buffalo Bill was a good stage actor.

☐ d. Buffalo Bill should have toured Europe with his show.                    _____

**Clarifying Devices**   **5**   A "re-creation of Custer's Last Stand" refers to

☐ a. an acting out of the battle.

☐ b. an actual battle.

☐ c. a retelling of the story, but with a new ending.

☐ d. a building of a battle monument.                    _____

**Vocabulary in Context**   **6**   In this passage, <u>exploits</u> means

☐ a. killings.

☐ b. childhood adventures.

☐ c. daring deeds.

☐ d. construction of the railroad.                    _____

**Add your scores for questions 1–6. Enter the total here and on the graph on page 219.**     Total Score     _____

# 95 A Terrible Year

Many people remember horrible years in their lives, times when nothing seemed to go right. Sometimes countries can have years like this too.

To many Americans, 1968 was a truly terrible year for their country. More and more people were protesting the government's involvement in Vietnam. African Americans were continuing to demand equal rights as citizens. The country was in a tense, hostile mood.

In early April, the Reverend Martin Luther King, Jr., went to Memphis to lead a protest march of black sanitation workers. On the evening of April 4, as he was leaving his motel to go to dinner, he was shot and killed by an assassin. This senseless death provoked riots in many cities.

Just two months later, another political assassination took place. Robert Kennedy, brother of the late President, had decided to run for president himself. Many people saw Kennedy as a leader who might bring the country together. Kennedy won the California primary and had just made a victory speech. Then he too was shot.

These two violent deaths frightened many people. But the Democratic National Convention in August was a final outrage. While the delegates bitterly debated to select a candidate, out on the Chicago streets police were clashing with antiwar protesters. Once again, violence ruled.

Looking at the United States today, it may be hard to believe this year of trouble occurred. But those who lived through it will never forget it.

| Main Idea | 1 | Answer | Score |
|---|---|---|---|
| | **Mark the *main idea*** | M | 15 |
| | **Mark the statement that is *too broad*** | B | 5 |
| | **Mark the statement that is *too narrow*** | N | 5 |
| | a. Everyone has bad years in their lives. | ☐ | _____ |
| | b. Three violent events made 1968 a terrible year. | ☐ | _____ |
| | c. Robert Kennedy had been a candidate for president. | ☐ | _____ |

**Subject Matter**     **2**     Another good title for this passage might be
- ☐ a. Two Murders in Two Months.
- ☐ b. A Year of Senseless Violence.
- ☐ c. History in the Making.
- ☐ d. The Beginning of the Civil Rights Movement.     _____

**Supporting Details**     **3**     Martin Luther King, Jr., was killed in
- ☐ a. New York.
- ☐ b. Chicago.
- ☐ c. California.
- ☐ d. Memphis.     _____

**Conclusion**     **4**     The author seems to feel that life in the United States
- ☐ a. has always been violent.
- ☐ b. has been more peaceful since 1968.
- ☐ c. is never good for African Americans.
- ☐ d. is a constant battle between the rich and the poor.     _____

**Clarifying Devices**     **5**     The main idea of this passage is developed through
- ☐ a. three examples.
- ☐ b. biographies of King and Kennedy.
- ☐ c. vivid descriptions of locations.
- ☐ d. questions and answers.     _____

**Vocabulary in Context**     **6**     <u>Assassination</u> means
- ☐ a. murder of a well-known person.
- ☐ b. crime.
- ☐ c. protest.
- ☐ d. plot involving several people.     _____

**Add your scores for questions 1–6. Enter the total here and on the graph on page 219.**     **Total Score**     _____

# 96 A Gift to the People

Many Americans take national parks for granted. Few people realize how these beautiful sites became public property.

Early in the country's history, federal policymakers began to recognize the importance of setting aside land. They saw more and more people moving west. They feared that this movement would cause some of our most beautiful scenery to be destroyed. In 1832, the government chose the first natural area to be legally protected. This was the Hot Springs region in Arkansas. It was a spot that many people had been visiting to seek cures for arthritis.

The first actual national park was Yellowstone. It was established in 1872. For years, people in the East had heard stories of this area. In it were places where hot water and steam supposedly spouted out of the earth. Then explorers returned with photographs showing that such an area really existed. And Congress was ready to protect it. They set the land aside "for the benefit and enjoyment of the people." A second national park, Yosemite, was established in 1890. Its purpose was to protect a beautiful area of California from overdevelopment.

In 1901, <u>conservationist</u> Theodore Roosevelt became president. The number of national parks began to grow rapidly. Today there are over fifty of them, and people visit in great numbers. In fact, many parks are almost too popular. There is sometimes serious overcrowding. Also, too many people use the parks carelessly. As a result, some are experiencing serious damage. Lands set aside for all generations of Americans now run the risk of being destroyed.

**Main Idea**    1

|  | Answer | Score |
|---|:---:|:---:|
| Mark the *main idea* | M | 15 |
| Mark the statement that is *too broad* | B | 5 |
| Mark the statement that is *too narrow* | N | 5 |

a. Countries need places like national parks. ☐ _____

b. First established in the late 1800s, national parks have become more and more popular. ☐ _____

c. The United States now has over fifty national parks. ☐ _____

**Subject Matter** 2 Another title for this passage could be
- ☐ a. The National Parks of the United States.
- ☐ b. National Parks Around the World.
- ☐ c. The Establishment of Yellowstone Park.
- ☐ d. How Overcrowding Is Harming the National Parks.

_____

**Supporting Details** 3 The first national park was at
- ☐ a. Hot Springs.
- ☐ b. Yellowstone.
- ☐ c. Yosemite.
- ☐ d. the Grand Canyon.

_____

**Conclusion** 4 The reader can conclude that
- ☐ a. Theodore Roosevelt supported national parks.
- ☐ b. Yellowstone became popular as soon as it was founded.
- ☐ c. the government did not want to establish Yosemite as a park.
- ☐ d. soon people will not be allowed to use the national parks at all.

_____

**Clarifying Devices** 5 The information in this passage is presented
- ☐ a. in spatial order.
- ☐ b. in chronological order.
- ☐ c. in cause and effect order.
- ☐ d. from a late date to an earlier date.

_____

**Vocabulary in Context** 6 A conservationist is a person who
- ☐ a. grabs land for himself or herself.
- ☐ b. tries to protect the land.
- ☐ c. is the first to settle in an area.
- ☐ d. raises crops in order to feed a family.

_____

**Add your scores for questions 1–6. Enter the total here and on the graph on page 219.**  **Total Score**

_____

# 97 Animals Beware!

The history of executions is not a pleasant story. Executions that took place in the Middle Ages were especially bizarre. For example, many of the victims were animals. It was common for animals ranging from insects to wolves to be <u>tried</u> publicly. Ecclesiastical courts, which were courts that represented the church, would often decide that certain animals were witches or heretics. The court's punishment was often excommunication (expulsion from the church), torture, or death. One of the last animal executions took place in France in 1740. The presiding judge ordered that a cow be hung by its neck because he believed it to be a sorcerer.

One of the most striking stories recorded concerned a pig that lived six hundred years ago. This pig had killed a little girl—or at least this is what the judge was told. For its crime, the pig was to have its legs mutilated, and then it was to be hanged. In preparation for this grisly end, the pig was dressed up in a child's jacket and ceremoniously dragged into the public square. The execution was called a "six sous" job because the executioner was given six French sous, or pennies, to buy a pair of gloves in order to keep his hands clean during the execution.

| Main Idea | 1 | | Answer | Score |
|---|---|---|---|---|
| | Mark the *main idea* | | M | 15 |
| | Mark the statement that is *too broad* | | B | 5 |
| | Mark the statement that is *too narrow* | | N | 5 |

a. In the Middle Ages, pigs were tried for crimes. ☐ _____

b. Killing animals was common during the Middle Ages. ☐ _____

c. Centuries ago, animals were often tried and executed. ☐ _____

**Score 15 points for each correct answer.**                    **Score**

**Subject Matter**    2    The subject of the passage is
☐ a. animals.
☐ b. animal executions.
☐ c. hangings.
☐ d. the Middle Ages.                    _____

**Supporting**    3    About 600 years ago, people believed that
**Details**              animals could commit
☐ a. larceny.
☐ b. adultery.
☐ c. robbery.
☐ d. murder.                    _____

**Conclusion**    4    It is obvious that many people of the past were
☐ a. unhappy.
☐ b. peaceful.
☐ c. superstitious.
☐ d. angry.                    _____

**Clarifying**    5    The phrase "One of the most striking stories" is
**Devices**              an indication that the story that follows will be
☐ a. very difficult.
☐ b. especially surprising.
☐ c. hard to take.
☐ d. very beautiful.                    _____

**Vocabulary**    6    In this passage <u>tried</u> means
**in Context**
☐ a. given a trial.
☐ b. give a hard time.
☐ c. saw how it worked.
☐ d. melted for fat.                    _____

**Add your scores for questions 1–6. Enter the total here**    **Total**
**and on the graph on page 219.**                    **Score**    _____

# 98 The Day of the Dead

Perhaps you've heard of the Mexican celebration of the Day of the Dead. And perhaps, because it occurs around the same time, you thought this holiday was pretty much the same as Halloween. But if you thought this, you would be wrong.

The Day of the Dead is a time to remember departed relatives and friends, but not in a sad or morbid way. Families get together to share happy memories of the past, to feast on special foods, and to put flowers and other gifts on the graves of loved ones. Many people believe that on the Day of the Dead the spirits of the dead will return to join the living. This holiday is popular not only in Mexico. It is also celebrated in many regions of the United States and Central America. Festivities vary from location to location.

The origins of the Day of the Dead can be traced to the Aztec Indians. These early inhabitants of Mexico set aside an entire month to celebrate the dead. When the Spanish invaded, they changed the date of the holiday to coincide with the Catholic All Saints Day and All Souls Day, November 1st and 2nd.

One reason people sometimes confuse the Day of the Dead with Halloween is because skeletons are so much a part of the celebrations. One popular skeletal figure is Katarina, who wears a dress and plumed hat. Skulls and skeletons also decorate many baked goods and sugar candies prepared for the day.

| Main Idea | 1 | | Answer | Score |
|---|---|---|---|---|
| | Mark the *main idea* | | M | 15 |
| | Mark the statement that is *too broad* | | B | 5 |
| | Mark the statement that is *too narrow* | | N | 5 |

a. The Day of the Dead celebration involves interesting customs and traditions. ☐ _____

b. Skeletons are an important part of the celebration. ☐ _____

c. Many holidays honor the dead. ☐ _____

**Score 15 points for each correct answer.**                    **Score**

**Subject Matter**   **2**   This passage is mostly about
- ☐ a. things that are done to celebrate the Day of the Dead.
- ☐ b. differences between Halloween and the Day of the Dead.
- ☐ c. how the Day of the Dead became a holiday.
- ☐ d. people's fear of dying.                    _____

**Supporting Details**   **3**   The Day of the Dead is celebrated
- ☐ a. only in Mexico.
- ☐ b. throughout Europe.
- ☐ c. only in Central America.
- ☐ d. in Mexico, Central America, and the United States.                    _____

**Conclusion**   **4**   From this passage one can conclude that the Day of the Dead is
- ☐ a. a sad holiday.
- ☐ b. a joyful holiday.
- ☐ c. celebrated only by religious people.
- ☐ d. celebrated mostly by children.                    _____

**Clarifying Devices**   **5**   The word "But" at the end of the first paragraph signals
- ☐ a. a similarity.
- ☐ b. a contrast.
- ☐ c. an argument.
- ☐ d. a description.                    _____

**Vocabulary in Context**   **6**   The word <u>coincide</u> is used to mean
- ☐ a. overrun.
- ☐ b. replace.
- ☐ c. happen at the same time.
- ☐ d. happen later.                    _____

**Add your scores for questions 1–6. Enter the total here and on the graph on page 219.**     **Total Score**     _____

# 99  The Greatest Jumper

The world's best jumpers all come from Australia. Most Olympic athletes train for years before they succeed in making a twenty-foot long jump. But the kangaroo, the greatest jumper on earth, can travel in twenty-foot leaps, moving almost as fast as a car on the highway!

The kangaroo's build enables it to travel at this high speed for extremely long distances without stopping. Its small head and short front feet <u>reduce</u> resistance to the wind, giving the animal a streamlined appearance. All of the kangaroo's weight is concentrated on the back of its body—in the thick, long tail and the long hindquarters. The animal can sit on its tail as if it were a chair or use it to maintain balance during long bounds. The kangaroo's hind feet, which are like springboards when it jumps, can be as long as ten inches from heel to toe.

Another interesting aspect of the kangaroo is the strength in its front feet. If those front feet were to be dressed in boxing gloves, the kangaroo could probably win a boxing match. It is known that the kangaroo can deliver strong punches; it can also hop around and completely exhaust an opponent. But despite advantages in speed and endurance, the kangaroo will not hurt other animals and will eat only vegetables. And although the kangaroo can leap over five-foot fences as if they were nothing, this surprising animal really can't walk.

**Main Idea**   1 ───────────────────────────

|  | Answer | Score |
|---|---|---|
| **Mark the _main idea_** | M | 15 |
| **Mark the statement that is _too broad_** | B | 5 |
| **Mark the statement that is _too narrow_** | N | 5 |
| a.  Some animals can travel very fast. | ☐ | _____ |
| b.  The kangaroo's body allows it to do some amazing things. | ☐ | _____ |
| c.  The kangaroo could be a good boxer. | ☐ | _____ |

**Score 15 points for each correct answer.**          **Score**

**Subject Matter**   **2**   This passage is concerned with
☐ a. runners and boxers.
☐ b. the kangaroo.
☐ c. Australia.
☐ d. jumping over fences.          _____

**Supporting Details**   **3**   Although the kangaroo probably could beat a person in boxing, it can't
☐ a. walk.
☐ b. race as fast as a car.
☐ c. jump long distances.
☐ d. jump over fences.          _____

**Conclusion**   **4**   The kangaroo can jump so rapidly because its
☐ a. survival depends on speed.
☐ b. body is ideally built for it.
☐ c. parents trained it.
☐ d. constant practice developed strong muscles.          _____

**Clarifying Devices**   **5**   The author develops the main idea by
☐ a. using examples.
☐ b. telling separate kangaroo stories.
☐ c. citing research data.
☐ d. describing the countryside in Australia.          _____

**Vocabulary in Context**   **6**   Reduce in this passage means
☐ a. cut down on.
☐ b. lose weight.
☐ c. shrink.
☐ d. increase.          _____

**Add your scores for questions 1–6. Enter the total here and on the graph on page 219.**

**Total Score**          _____

# 100 The Ageless Wonder

When Bill Veeck, owner of the Cleveland Indians baseball team, signed aging Leroy "Satchel" Paige, Veeck was accused of creating a cheap publicity stunt. It was the sort of move a lot of people thought would be bad for the team and bad for baseball. Paige had been a legendary pitcher in the Negro Leagues, so what was the objection? His age.

Paige was always secretive about the date of his birth, but at the time he was about to pitch his first major league game, most estimates put him at around forty-two years old. During his twenty years in the Negro Leagues, he had been the finest pitcher those leagues had ever seen. But the attitude in Cleveland was that he had been great in his day but had surely outlived his effectiveness.

The night Paige played in his first game with Cleveland, 51,013 fans flocked into Comiskey Park in Chicago to see what the old man could do against the powerful White Sox. Satch was in complete control. He gave up only five hits, and the Indians beat the Sox 5–0. A week later, Paige beat the Sox again in front of still another record-breaking crowd in the Indians' home stadium.

Veeck's faith in Paige had certainly been <u>vindicated</u>. The Indians won the American League Championship that year, and the contributions of the "Ageless Wonder," Satchel Paige, were responsible for a large part of their success.

| Main Idea | 1 | Answer | Score |
|---|---|---|---|
| | Mark the *main idea* | M | 15 |
| | Mark the statement that is *too broad* | B | 5 |
| | Mark the statement that is *too narrow* | N | 5 |

a. Despite his age, Paige proved to be an asset to the Cleveland Indians. ☐ _____

b. Many people thought Paige was too old to be in the Major Leagues. ☐ _____

c. Few people over forty play in the major leagues. ☐ _____

**Score 15 points for each correct answer.**        Score

**Subject Matter**   2   The passage is mainly about
- [ ] a. the Negro League in baseball.
- [ ] b. Satchel Paige's early career.
- [ ] c. how Paige proved himself in the majors.
- [ ] d. Paige's first game in the majors.        _____

**Supporting Details**   3   There was a crowd at Comiskey Park because
- [ ] a. Satchel Paige had never pitched before.
- [ ] b. Paige was very popular in Chicago.
- [ ] c. it was the American League playoffs.
- [ ] d. Satchel Paige was pitching for the first time in the major leagues.        _____

**Conclusion**   4   The use of the phrase "cheap publicity stunt" in the first paragraph suggests that people believed
- [ ] a. Veeck didn't expect Paige to be good, but signed him to get publicity for the team.
- [ ] b. Bill Veeck didn't pay Paige very much.
- [ ] c. Paige wasn't really going to pitch, but was just going to be an attraction.
- [ ] d. publicity was all Paige cared about.        _____

**Clarifying Devices**   5   The method used by the writer in the passage is
- [ ] a. logical argument.
- [ ] b. telling a story.
- [ ] c. questions and answers.
- [ ] d. exaggeration.        _____

**Vocabulary in Context**   6   The best definition for the word <u>vindicated</u>, as used in the passage, is
- [ ] a. corrected.
- [ ] b. proved wrong.
- [ ] c. proved right.
- [ ] d. widely publicized.        _____

**Add your scores for questions 1–6. Enter the total here and on the graph on page 219.**        Total Score        _____

# Answer Key

| | | | | | | | |
|---|---|---|---|---|---|---|---|
| Passage 1: | 1a. **N** | 1b. **M** | 1c. **B** | 2. **b** | 3. **c** | 4. **d** | 5. **b** | 6. **b** |
| Passage 2: | 1a. **B** | 1b. **M** | 1c. **N** | 2. **c** | 3. **b** | 4. **a** | 5. **c** | 6. **a** |
| Passage 3: | 1a. **N** | 1b. **M** | 1c. **B** | 2. **b** | 3. **d** | 4. **a** | 5. **c** | 6. **b** |
| Passage 4: | 1a. **B** | 1b. **M** | 1c. **N** | 2. **d** | 3. **a** | 4. **c** | 5. **b** | 6. **c** |
| Passage 5: | 1a. **B** | 1b. **M** | 1c. **N** | 2. **c** | 3. **d** | 4. **c** | 5. **b** | 6. **a** |
| Passage 6: | 1a. **B** | 1b. **N** | 1c. **M** | 2. **a** | 3. **b** | 4. **d** | 5. **b** | 6. **d** |
| Passage 7: | 1a. **N** | 1b. **B** | 1c. **M** | 2. **b** | 3. **c** | 4. **a** | 5. **b** | 6. **d** |
| Passage 8: | 1a. **N** | 1b. **B** | 1c. **M** | 2. **c** | 3. **c** | 4. **b** | 5. **c** | 6. **c** |
| Passage 9: | 1a. **M** | 1b. **B** | 1c. **N** | 2. **b** | 3. **c** | 4. **a** | 5. **b** | 6. **a** |
| Passage 10: | 1a. **M** | 1b. **B** | 1c. **N** | 2. **c** | 3. **d** | 4. **b** | 5. **c** | 6. **b** |
| Passage 11: | 1a. **B** | 1b. **N** | 1c. **M** | 2. **d** | 3. **a** | 4. **b** | 5. **d** | 6. **c** |
| Passage 12: | 1a. **M** | 1b. **N** | 1c. **B** | 2. **b** | 3. **c** | 4. **c** | 5. **a** | 6. **c** |
| Passage 13: | 1a. **B** | 1b. **M** | 1c. **N** | 2. **b** | 3. **a** | 4. **c** | 5. **c** | 6. **b** |
| Passage 14: | 1a. **N** | 1b. **M** | 1c. **B** | 2. **d** | 3. **d** | 4. **a** | 5. **c** | 6. **a** |
| Passage 15: | 1a. **N** | 1b. **B** | 1c. **M** | 2. **d** | 3. **c** | 4. **b** | 5. **d** | 6. **a** |
| Passage 16: | 1a. **M** | 1b. **N** | 1c. **B** | 2. **b** | 3. **d** | 4. **d** | 5. **c** | 6. **b** |
| Passage 17: | 1a. **M** | 1b. **N** | 1c. **B** | 2. **a** | 3. **c** | 4. **b** | 5. **c** | 6. **b** |
| Passage 18: | 1a. **M** | 1b. **N** | 1c. **B** | 2. **c** | 3. **c** | 4. **b** | 5. **b** | 6. **a** |
| Passage 19: | 1a. **M** | 1b. **B** | 1c. **N** | 2. **b** | 3. **c** | 4. **b** | 5. **a** | 6. **c** |
| Passage 20: | 1a. **M** | 1b. **B** | 1c. **N** | 2. **d** | 3. **a** | 4. **c** | 5. **a** | 6. **b** |

| Passage 21: | 1a. **M** | 1b. **N** | 1c. **B** | 2. **b** | 3. **d** | 4. **b** | 5. **d** | 6. **c** |
|---|---|---|---|---|---|---|---|---|
| Passage 22: | 1a. **B** | 1b. **M** | 1c. **N** | 2. **c** | 3. **d** | 4. **b** | 5. **a** | 6. **c** |
| Passage 23: | 1a. **B** | 1b. **M** | 1c. **N** | 2. **b** | 3. **d** | 4. **a** | 5. **c** | 6. **c** |
| Passage 24: | 1a. **B** | 1b. **M** | 1c. **N** | 2. **c** | 3. **a** | 4. **c** | 5. **a** | 6. **b** |
| Passage 25: | 1a. **B** | 1b. **M** | 1c. **N** | 2. **b** | 3. **c** | 4. **b** | 5. **d** | 6. **a** |
| Passage 26: | 1a. **M** | 1b. **N** | 1c. **B** | 2. **b** | 3. **b** | 4. **c** | 5. **d** | 6. **c** |
| Passage 27: | 1a. **M** | 1b. **N** | 1c. **B** | 2. **a** | 3. **b** | 4. **d** | 5. **b** | 6. **c** |
| Passage 28: | 1a. **B** | 1b. **M** | 1c. **N** | 2. **a** | 3. **c** | 4. **c** | 5. **b** | 6. **c** |
| Passage 29: | 1a. **B** | 1b. **N** | 1c. **M** | 2. **a** | 3. **c** | 4. **c** | 5. **b** | 6. **c** |
| Passage 30: | 1a. **M** | 1b. **B** | 1c. **N** | 2. **b** | 3. **c** | 4. **b** | 5. **c** | 6. **d** |
| Passage 31: | 1a. **M** | 1b. **N** | 1c. **B** | 2. **c** | 3. **c** | 4. **c** | 5. **c** | 6. **b** |
| Passage 32: | 1a. **B** | 1b. **N** | 1c. **M** | 2. **a** | 3. **b** | 4. **a** | 5. **b** | 6. **d** |
| Passage 33: | 1a. **B** | 1b. **N** | 1c. **M** | 2. **c** | 3. **d** | 4. **a** | 5. **b** | 6. **c** |
| Passage 34: | 1a. **N** | 1b. **M** | 1c. **B** | 2. **a** | 3. **d** | 4. **b** | 5. **c** | 6. **c** |
| Passage 35: | 1a. **M** | 1b. **B** | 1c. **N** | 2. **b** | 3. **c** | 4. **c** | 5. **a** | 6. **c** |
| Passage 36: | 1a. **N** | 1b. **M** | 1c. **B** | 2. **a** | 3. **c** | 4. **d** | 5. **a** | 6. **a** |
| Passage 37: | 1a. **B** | 1b. **M** | 1c. **N** | 2. **c** | 3. **a** | 4. **d** | 5. **c** | 6. **b** |
| Passage 38: | 1a. **N** | 1b. **B** | 1c. **M** | 2. **c** | 3. **a** | 4. **c** | 5. **d** | 6. **c** |
| Passage 39: | 1a. **M** | 1b. **N** | 1c. **B** | 2. **c** | 3. **b** | 4. **d** | 5. **a** | 6. **b** |
| Passage 40: | 1a. **M** | 1b. **B** | 1c. **N** | 2. **b** | 3. **c** | 4. **c** | 5. **b** | 6. **c** |

| Passage 41: | 1a. **B** | 1b. **M** | 1c. **N** | 2. **a** | 3. **b** | 4. **a** | 5. **a** | 6. **a** |
|---|---|---|---|---|---|---|---|---|
| Passage 42: | 1a. **N** | 1b. **B** | 1c. **M** | 2. **c** | 3. **c** | 4. **c** | 5. **c** | 6. **a** |
| Passage 43: | 1a. **M** | 1b. **N** | 1c. **B** | 2. **b** | 3. **d** | 4. **c** | 5. **c** | 6. **b** |
| Passage 44: | 1a. **B** | 1b. **N** | 1c. **M** | 2. **c** | 3. **c** | 4. **c** | 5. **a** | 6. **c** |
| Passage 45: | 1a. **M** | 1b. **N** | 1c. **B** | 2. **c** | 3. **b** | 4. **d** | 5. **a** | 6. **c** |
| Passage 46: | 1a. **N** | 1b. **M** | 1c. **B** | 2. **c** | 3. **d** | 4. **c** | 5. **d** | 6. **c** |
| Passage 47: | 1a. **B** | 1b. **M** | 1c. **N** | 2. **a** | 3. **d** | 4. **d** | 5. **b** | 6.**a** |
| Passage 48: | 1a. **M** | 1b. **B** | 1c. **N** | 2. **c** | 3. **b** | 4. **c** | 5. **a** | 6. **b** |
| Passage 49: | 1a. **M** | 1b. **B** | 1c. **N** | 2. **b** | 3. **b** | 4. **c** | 5. **a** | 6. **d** |
| Passage 50: | 1a. **N** | 1b. **B** | 1c. **M** | 2. **d** | 3. **c** | 4. **d** | 5. **a** | 6. **c** |
| Passage 51: | 1a. **M** | 1b. **B** | 1c. **N** | 2. **b** | 3. **b** | 4. **c** | 5. **a** | 6. **c** |
| Passage 52: | 1a. **B** | 1b. **M** | 1c. **N** | 2. **b** | 3. **d** | 4. **b** | 5.**b** | 6. **d** |
| Passage 53: | 1a. **B** | 1b. **M** | 1c. **N** | 2. **c** | 3. **b** | 4. **c** | 5. **a** | 6. **c** |
| Passage 54: | 1a. **N** | 1b. **M** | 1c. **B** | 2. **a** | 3. **c** | 4. **a** | 5. **b** | 6. **b** |
| Passage 55: | 1a. **M** | 1b. **N** | 1c. **B** | 2. **d** | 3. **c** | 4. **d** | 5. **b** | 6. **c** |
| Passage 56: | 1a. **B** | 1b. **N** | 1c. **M** | 2. **b** | 3. **b** | 4. **c** | 5. **b** | 6. **b** |
| Passage 57: | 1a. **B** | 1b. **N** | 1c. **M** | 2. **b** | 3. **d** | 4. **a** | 5. **c** | 6. **c** |
| Passage 58: | 1a. **B** | 1b. **M** | 1c. **N** | 2. **c** | 3. **d** | 4. **b** | 5. **d** | 6. **b** |
| Passage 59: | 1a. **M** | 1b. **B** | 1c. **N** | 2. **b** | 3. **a** | 4. **c** | 5. **c** | 6. **d** |
| Passage 60: | 1a. **M** | 1b. **N** | 1c. **B** | 2. **b** | 3. **d** | 4. **b** | 5. **c** | 6. **b** |

| Passage 61: | 1a. **B** | 1b. **M** | 1c. **N** | 2. **b** | 3. **b** | 4. **c** | 5. **d** | 6. **a** |
|---|---|---|---|---|---|---|---|---|
| Passage 62: | 1a. **M** | 1b. **B** | 1c. **N** | 2. **a** | 3. **c** | 4. **b** | 5. **b** | 6. **c** |
| Passage 63: | 1a. **B** | 1b. **N** | 1c. **M** | 2. **d** | 3. **c** | 4. **c** | 5. **a** | 6. **b** |
| Passage 64: | 1a. **B** | 1b. **M** | 1c. **N** | 2. **d** | 3. **c** | 4. **c** | 5. **b** | 6. **d** |
| Passage 65: | 1a. **M** | 1b. **N** | 1c. **B** | 2. **a** | 3. **c** | 4. **c** | 5. **a** | 6. **b** |
| Passage 66: | 1a. **M** | 1b. **N** | 1c. **B** | 2. **d** | 3. **d** | 4. **c** | 5. **b** | 6. **b** |
| Passage 67: | 1a. **B** | 1b. **N** | 1c. **M** | 2. **c** | 3. **c** | 4. **d** | 5. **a** | 6. **a** |
| Passage 68: | 1a. **M** | 1b. **N** | 1c. **B** | 2. **a** | 3. **c** | 4. **c** | 5. **a** | 6. **a** |
| Passage 69: | 1a. **B** | 1b. **M** | 1c. **N** | 2. **b** | 3. **a** | 4. **b** | 5. **b** | 6. **d** |
| Passage 70: | 1a. **M** | 1b. **N** | 1c. **B** | 2. **b** | 3. **b** | 4. **b** | 5. **c** | 6. **c** |
| Passage 71: | 1a. **N** | 1b. **B** | 1c. **M** | 2. **d** | 3. **d** | 4. **a** | 5. **a** | 6. **d** |
| Passage 72: | 1a. **M** | 1b. **N** | 1c. **B** | 2. **d** | 3. **c** | 4. **b** | 5. **a** | 6. **d** |
| Passage 73: | 1a. **N** | 1b. **B** | 1c. **M** | 2. **b** | 3. **d** | 4. **c** | 5. **a** | 6. **c** |
| Passage 74: | 1a. **B** | 1b. **M** | 1c. **N** | 2. **b** | 3. **c** | 4. **b** | 5. **b** | 6. **d** |
| Passage 75: | 1a. **B** | 1b. **M** | 1c. **N** | 2. **a** | 3. **c** | 4. **d** | 5. **a** | 6. **b** |
| Passage 76: | 1a. **B** | 1b. **M** | 1c. **N** | 2. **b** | 3. **d** | 4. **c** | 5. **b** | 6. **a** |
| Passage 77: | 1a. **M** | 1b. **N** | 1c. **B** | 2. **d** | 3. **b** | 4. **c** | 5. **d** | 6. **a** |
| Passage 78: | 1a. **M** | 1b. **N** | 1c. **B** | 2. **c** | 3. **b** | 4. **c** | 5. **a** | 6. **d** |
| Passage 79: | 1a. **M** | 1b. **B** | 1c. **N** | 2. **d** | 3. **a** | 4. **d** | 5. **d** | 6. **b** |
| Passage 80: | 1a. **B** | 1b. **M** | 1c. **N** | 2. **a** | 3. **b** | 4. **c** | 5. **a** | 6. **c** |

| Passage 81: | 1a. **B** | 1b. **M** | 1c. **N** | 2. **b** | 3. **d** | 4. **a** | 5. **d** | 6. **b** |
| Passage 82: | 1a. **N** | 1b. **B** | 1c. **M** | 2. **a** | 3. **b** | 4. **a** | 5. **d** | 6. **a** |
| Passage 83: | 1a. **B** | 1b. **M** | 1c. **N** | 2. **b** | 3. **a** | 4. **b** | 5. **a** | 6. **b** |
| Passage 84: | 1a. **N** | 1b. **B** | 1c. **M** | 2. **c** | 3. **c** | 4. **b** | 5. **a** | 6. **d** |
| Passage 85: | 1a. **M** | 1b. **B** | 1c. **N** | 2. **c** | 3. **c** | 4. **a** | 5. **b** | 6. **d** |
| Passage 86: | 1a. **M** | 1b. **B** | 1c. **N** | 2. **d** | 3. **b** | 4. **a** | 5. **b** | 6. **a** |
| Passage 87: | 1a. **N** | 1b. **B** | 1c. **M** | 2. **b** | 3. **a** | 4. **b** | 5. **c** | 6. **b** |
| Passage 88: | 1a. **N** | 1b. **B** | 1c. **M** | 2. **b** | 3. **d** | 4. **a** | 5. **c** | 6. **b** |
| Passage 89: | 1a. **M** | 1b. **B** | 1c. **N** | 2. **c** | 3. **b** | 4. **a** | 5. **b** | 6. **d** |
| Passage 90: | 1a. **B** | 1b. **M** | 1c. **N** | 2. **a** | 3. **d** | 4. **c** | 5. **a** | 6. **c** |
| Passage 91: | 1a. **B** | 1b. **M** | 1c. **N** | 2. **b** | 3. **a** | 4. **d** | 5. **a** | 6. **c** |
| Passage 92: | 1a. **M** | 1b. **B** | 1c. **N** | 2. **c** | 3. **c** | 4. **a** | 5. **b** | 6. **a** |
| Passage 93: | 1a. **B** | 1b. **N** | 1c. **M** | 2. **b** | 3. **c** | 4. **b** | 5. **b** | 6. **c** |
| Passage 94: | 1a. **M** | 1b. **N** | 1c. **B** | 2. **a** | 3. **b** | 4. **b** | 5. **a** | 6. **c** |
| Passage 95: | 1a. **B** | 1b. **M** | 1c. **N** | 2. **b** | 3. **d** | 4. **b** | 5. **a** | 6. **a** |
| Passage 96: | 1a. **B** | 1b. **M** | 1c. **N** | 2. **a** | 3. **b** | 4. **a** | 5. **b** | 6. **b** |
| Passage 97: | 1a. **N** | 1b. **B** | 1c. **M** | 2. **b** | 3. **d** | 4. **c** | 5. **b** | 6. **a** |
| Passage 98: | 1a. **M** | 1b. **N** | 1c. **B** | 2. **a** | 3. **d** | 4. **b** | 5. **b** | 6. **c** |
| Passage 99: | 1a. **B** | 1b. **M** | 1c. **N** | 2. **b** | 3. **a** | 4. **b** | 5. **a** | 6. **a** |
| Passage 100: | 1a. **M** | 1b. **N** | 1c. **B** | 2. **c** | 3. **d** | 4. **a** | 5. **b** | 6. **c** |

# Diagnostic Chart (For Student Correction)

**Directions:** For each passage, write your answers to the left of the dotted line in the blocks for each skill category. Then correct your answers using the Answer Key. If your answer is correct, do not make any more marks in the block. If your answer is incorrect, write the letter of the correct answer to the right of the dotted line.

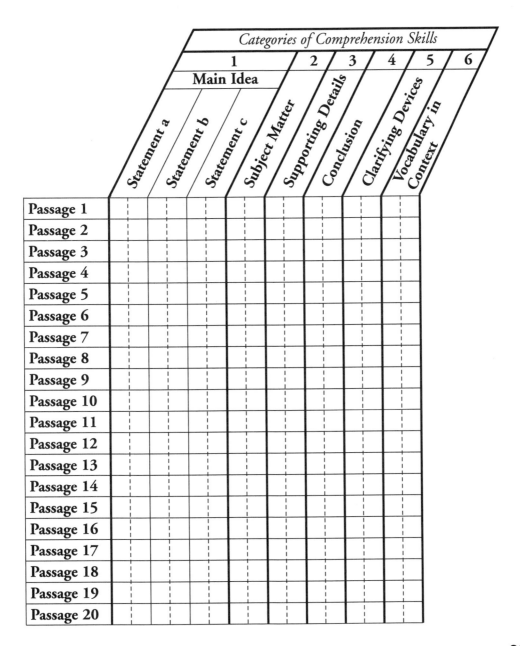

| | | Categories of Comprehension Skills | | | | | | | |
|---|---|---|---|---|---|---|---|---|---|
| | **1** Main Idea | | | **2** | **3** | | **4** | **5** | **6** |
| | Statement a | Statement b | Statement c | Subject Matter | Supporting Details | Conclusion | Clarifying Devices | Vocabulary in Context | |
| Passage 1 | | | | | | | | | |
| Passage 2 | | | | | | | | | |
| Passage 3 | | | | | | | | | |
| Passage 4 | | | | | | | | | |
| Passage 5 | | | | | | | | | |
| Passage 6 | | | | | | | | | |
| Passage 7 | | | | | | | | | |
| Passage 8 | | | | | | | | | |
| Passage 9 | | | | | | | | | |
| Passage 10 | | | | | | | | | |
| Passage 11 | | | | | | | | | |
| Passage 12 | | | | | | | | | |
| Passage 13 | | | | | | | | | |
| Passage 14 | | | | | | | | | |
| Passage 15 | | | | | | | | | |
| Passage 16 | | | | | | | | | |
| Passage 17 | | | | | | | | | |
| Passage 18 | | | | | | | | | |
| Passage 19 | | | | | | | | | |
| Passage 20 | | | | | | | | | |

## Diagnostic Chart: Passages 21–40

**Directions:** For each passage, write your answers to the left of the dotted line in the blocks for each skill category. Then correct your answers using the Answer Key. If your answer is correct, do not make any more marks in the block. If your answer is incorrect, write the letter of the correct answer to the right of the dotted line.

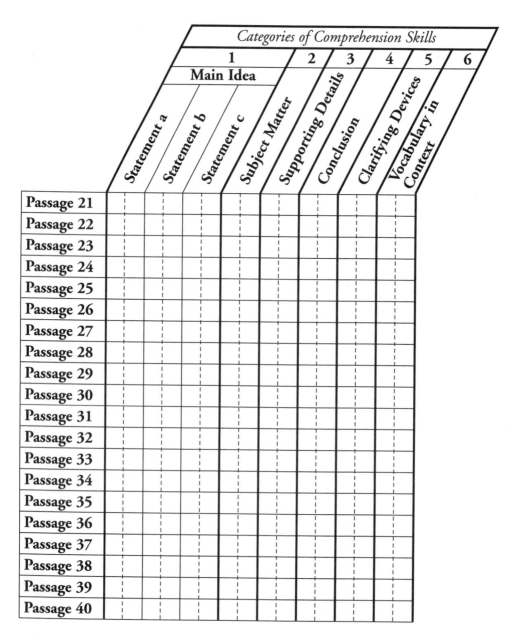

| | Categories of Comprehension Skills | | | | | | | | |
|---|---|---|---|---|---|---|---|---|---|
| | 1 Main Idea | | | | 2 | 3 | 4 | 5 | 6 |
| | Statement a | Statement b | Statement c | Subject Matter | Supporting Details | Conclusion | Clarifying Devices | Vocabulary in Context | |
| Passage 21 | | | | | | | | | |
| Passage 22 | | | | | | | | | |
| Passage 23 | | | | | | | | | |
| Passage 24 | | | | | | | | | |
| Passage 25 | | | | | | | | | |
| Passage 26 | | | | | | | | | |
| Passage 27 | | | | | | | | | |
| Passage 28 | | | | | | | | | |
| Passage 29 | | | | | | | | | |
| Passage 30 | | | | | | | | | |
| Passage 31 | | | | | | | | | |
| Passage 32 | | | | | | | | | |
| Passage 33 | | | | | | | | | |
| Passage 34 | | | | | | | | | |
| Passage 35 | | | | | | | | | |
| Passage 36 | | | | | | | | | |
| Passage 37 | | | | | | | | | |
| Passage 38 | | | | | | | | | |
| Passage 39 | | | | | | | | | |
| Passage 40 | | | | | | | | | |

## Diagnostic Chart: Passages 41–60

**Directions:** For each passage, write your answers to the left of the dotted line in the blocks for each skill category. Then correct your answers using the Answer Key. If your answer is correct, do not make any more marks in the block. If your answer is incorrect, write the letter of the correct answer to the right of the dotted line.

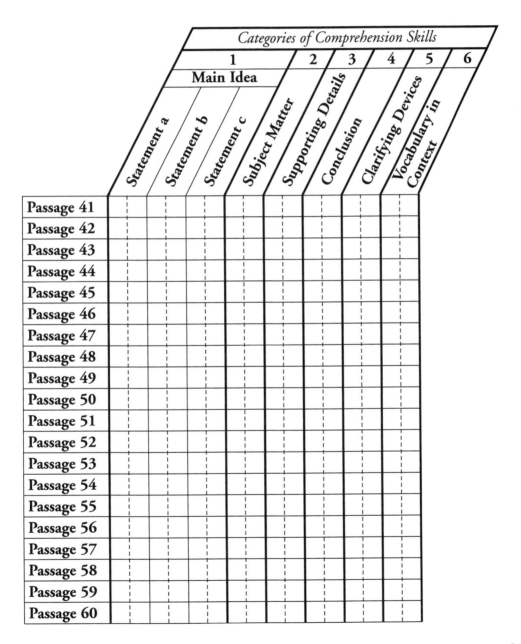

| | Categories of Comprehension Skills | | | | | | | |
|---|---|---|---|---|---|---|---|---|
| | 1 Main Idea | | | 2 | 3 | 4 | 5 | 6 |
| | Statement a | Statement b | Statement c | Subject Matter | Supporting Details | Conclusion | Clarifying Devices | Vocabulary in Context |
| Passage 41 | | | | | | | | |
| Passage 42 | | | | | | | | |
| Passage 43 | | | | | | | | |
| Passage 44 | | | | | | | | |
| Passage 45 | | | | | | | | |
| Passage 46 | | | | | | | | |
| Passage 47 | | | | | | | | |
| Passage 48 | | | | | | | | |
| Passage 49 | | | | | | | | |
| Passage 50 | | | | | | | | |
| Passage 51 | | | | | | | | |
| Passage 52 | | | | | | | | |
| Passage 53 | | | | | | | | |
| Passage 54 | | | | | | | | |
| Passage 55 | | | | | | | | |
| Passage 56 | | | | | | | | |
| Passage 57 | | | | | | | | |
| Passage 58 | | | | | | | | |
| Passage 59 | | | | | | | | |
| Passage 60 | | | | | | | | |

## Diagnostic Chart: Passages 61–80

**Directions:** For each passage, write your answers to the left of the dotted line in the blocks for each skill category. Then correct your answers using the Answer Key. If your answer is correct, do not make any more marks in the block. If your answer is incorrect, write the letter of the correct answer to the right of the dotted line.

| | Categories of Comprehension Skills | | | | | | | | |
| --- | --- | --- | --- | --- | --- | --- | --- | --- | --- |
| | **1** Main Idea | | | | **2** | **3** | **4** | **5** | **6** |
| | Statement a | Statement b | Statement c | Subject Matter | Supporting Details | Conclusion | Clarifying Devices | Vocabulary in Context | |
| Passage 61 | | | | | | | | | |
| Passage 62 | | | | | | | | | |
| Passage 63 | | | | | | | | | |
| Passage 64 | | | | | | | | | |
| Passage 65 | | | | | | | | | |
| Passage 66 | | | | | | | | | |
| Passage 67 | | | | | | | | | |
| Passage 68 | | | | | | | | | |
| Passage 69 | | | | | | | | | |
| Passage 70 | | | | | | | | | |
| Passage 71 | | | | | | | | | |
| Passage 72 | | | | | | | | | |
| Passage 73 | | | | | | | | | |
| Passage 74 | | | | | | | | | |
| Passage 75 | | | | | | | | | |
| Passage 76 | | | | | | | | | |
| Passage 77 | | | | | | | | | |
| Passage 78 | | | | | | | | | |
| Passage 79 | | | | | | | | | |
| Passage 80 | | | | | | | | | |

## Diagnostic Chart: Passages 81–100

**Directions:** For each passage, write your answers to the left of the dotted line in the blocks for each skill category. Then correct your answers using the Answer Key. If your answer is correct, do not make any more marks in the block. If your answer is incorrect, write the letter of the correct answer to the right of the dotted line.

| | Categories of Comprehension Skills | | | | | | | | |
| | 1 Main Idea | | | | 2 | 3 | 4 | 5 | 6 |
| | Statement a | Statement b | Statement c | Subject Matter | Supporting Details | Conclusion | Clarifying Devices | Vocabulary in Context | |
| Passage 81 | | | | | | | | | |
| Passage 82 | | | | | | | | | |
| Passage 83 | | | | | | | | | |
| Passage 84 | | | | | | | | | |
| Passage 85 | | | | | | | | | |
| Passage 86 | | | | | | | | | |
| Passage 87 | | | | | | | | | |
| Passage 88 | | | | | | | | | |
| Passage 89 | | | | | | | | | |
| Passage 90 | | | | | | | | | |
| Passage 91 | | | | | | | | | |
| Passage 92 | | | | | | | | | |
| Passage 93 | | | | | | | | | |
| Passage 94 | | | | | | | | | |
| Passage 95 | | | | | | | | | |
| Passage 96 | | | | | | | | | |
| Passage 97 | | | | | | | | | |
| Passage 98 | | | | | | | | | |
| Passage 99 | | | | | | | | | |
| Passage 100 | | | | | | | | | |

# Progress Graph

**Directions:** Write your Total Score for each passage in the comprehension score box under the number of the passage. Then plot your score on the graph itself by putting a small *x* on the line directly above the number of the passage, across from the score you got for that passage. As you mark your score for each passage, graph your progress by drawing a line to connect the *x*'s.

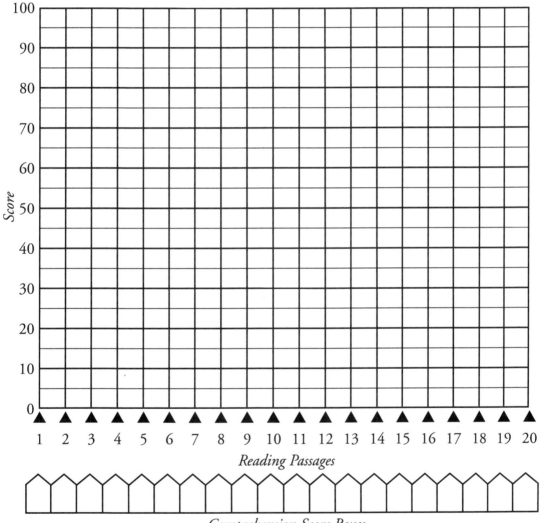

Reading Passages

Comprehension Score Boxes

*Progress Graph: Passages 21–40*

**Directions:** Write your Total Score for each passage in the comprehension score box under the number of the passage. Then plot your score on the graph itself by putting a small *x* on the line directly above the number of the passage, across from the score you got for that passage. As you mark your score for each passage, graph your progress by drawing a line to connect the *x*'s.

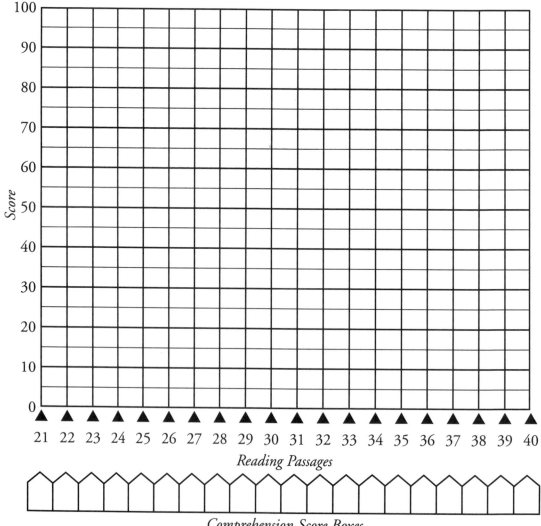

Comprehension Score Boxes

## Progress Graph: Passages 41–60

**Directions:** Write your Total Score for each passage in the comprehension score box under the number of the passage. Then plot your score on the graph itself by putting a small *x* on the line directly above the number of the passage, across from the score you got for that passage. As you mark your score for each passage, graph your progress by drawing a line to connect the *x*'s.

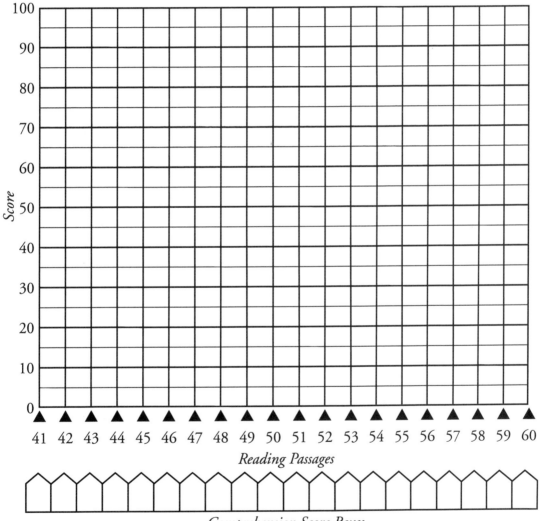

Comprehension Score Boxes

## Progress Graph: Passages 61–80

**Directions:** Write your Total Score for each passage in the comprehension score box under the number of the passage. Then plot your score on the graph itself by putting a small *x* on the line directly above the number of the passage, across from the score you got for that passage. As you mark your score for each passage, graph your progress by drawing a line to connect the *x*'s.

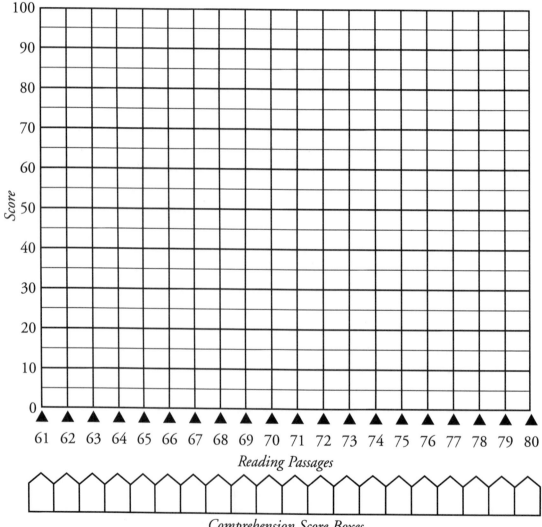

*Reading Passages*

*Comprehension Score Boxes*

*Progress Graph: Passages 81–100*

**Directions:** Write your Total Score for each passage in the comprehension score box under the number of the passage. Then plot your score on the graph itself by putting a small *x* on the line directly above the number of the passage, across from the score you got for that passage. As you mark your score for each passage, graph your progress by drawing a line to connect the *x*'s.

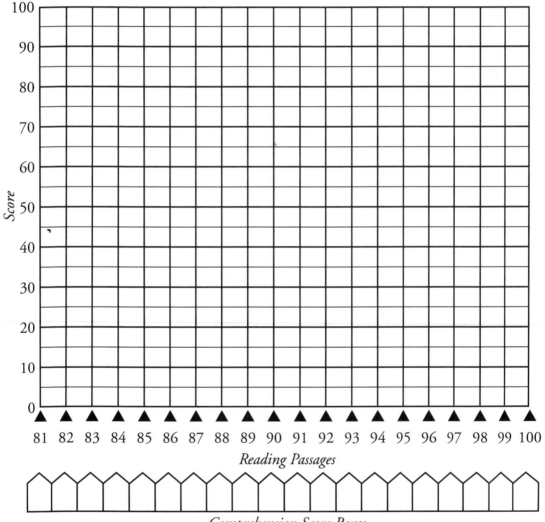

*Reading Passages*

*Comprehension Score Boxes*